VOLUME 4

# ALL-AMERICAN COOKING

® Landoll, Inc.

Ashland, Ohio 44805

Created and manufactured by arrangement with Ideals Publishing Corp.

**Printed in Canada**

# Contents

# Beverages

## Egg Nog

Makes 12 servings

**10 eggs, separated**
**1½ cups sugar**
**1 quart milk**
**½ cup heavy cream**
**½ teaspoon vanilla**
**¾ cup brandy**
**1 cup light rum**
**Nutmeg**

In a large mixing bowl, beat egg yolks until foamy. Add sugar; continue beating until mixture is lemon-colored. Stir in milk and cream. With clean beaters, beat egg whites in a separate bowl until stiff. Gradually beat in vanilla, then brandy and rum. Fold into milk mixture. Sprinkle with nutmeg.

## Mint Julep

Makes 1 serving

**6 mint leaves**
**1 teaspoon powdered sugar**
**2 teaspoons water**
**2¼ ounces bourbon**
**Orange slice**
**Mint sprig**

Place mint leaves in a 12-ounce tumbler. Add sugar and water; stir until sugar dissolves. Add bourbon and enough ice to fill the tumbler. Stir until outside of tumbler is frosted. Garnish with an orange slice and a sprig of mint.

## Tea Punch

Makes 24 servings

**2 cups strong tea**
**4 cups ginger ale**
**2 cups orange juice**
**2 cups cranberry juice**
**2 cups apple juice**
**Sugar to taste**
**Orange slices**
**Pineapple chunks**

Just before serving, stir together first 6 ingredients. Pour over an ice block in a punch bowl. Garnish with orange slices and pineapple chunks.

# Sangria

Makes 6 servings

**2 cups fresh orange juice**
**8 tablespoons fresh lemon juice**
**5 tablespoons superfine sugar**
**Ice cubes**
**Club soda**
**Dry red wine**
**¼ cup Maraschino cherries**
**6 orange slices**

In a small bowl, stir together orange juice, lemon juice, and sugar until blended. Pour equal amounts of the juice mixture into 6 ice-filled glasses. Fill ⅔ full with club soda. Add dry red wine to taste. Garnish each serving with cherries and an orange slice.

# Tomato Energizer

Makes 8 servings

**4 eggs**
**4 cups tomato juice**
**½ teaspoon salt**
**½ teaspoon Worcestershire sauce**
**Dash Tabasco sauce**

In a mixing bowl or blender, beat together all ingredients just until blended.

# Brunch Punch

Makes 20 servings

**6 quarts black coffee at room temperature**
**¾ cup sugar or to taste**
**1 tablespoon vanilla**
**½ teaspoon nutmeg**
**½ teaspoon cinnamon**
**1 quart heavy cream**
**1 quart coffee ice cream**
**1 quart vanilla ice cream**

In a punch bowl, stir together coffee and sugar until sugar dissolves. Stir in vanilla and spices. In a separate bowl, beat heavy cream until soft peaks form. Blend cream into coffee. Break ice cream into pieces with a spoon; add to coffee mixture.

# Cappucino

Makes 4 servings

**2 cups very strong coffee**
**2 cups milk**
**2 tablespoons sugar**
**Cinnamon**
**Nutmeg**

In a medium saucepan over medium heat, bring coffee, milk, and sugar to a simmer. Remove from heat. Beat until mixture is foamy. Pour into individual coffee cups. Sprinkle with cinnamon and nutmeg.

# Breads & Pastries

## Bacon Corn Bread

Makes 8 servings

**1½ cups yellow cornmeal**
**1 cup all-purpose flour**
**⅓ cup sugar**
**3 strips bacon, crisp-cooked and crumbled**
**1 tablespoon baking powder**
**½ teaspoon salt**
**2 eggs**
**1½ cups milk**
**4 tablespoons bacon drippings**

Preheat oven to 400° F. Grease a 9-inch square baking pan or cornbread pan. In a mixing bowl, stir together cornmeal, flour, sugar, bacon, baking powder, and salt. In a separate bowl, beat eggs, milk, and 4 tablespoons bacon drippings until blended. Add to dry ingredients. Stir just until dry ingredients are moistened. Pour into prepared pan. Bake for 30 minutes or until a wooden pick inserted near the center comes out clean.

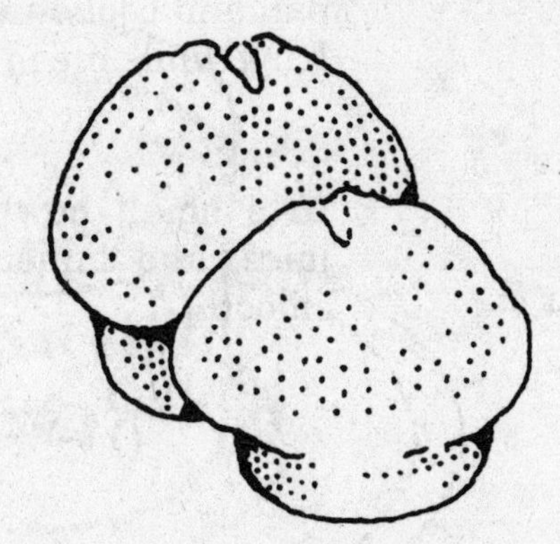

## Soft Rolls

Makes 2 dozen rolls

**1 package active dry yeast**
**1 cup warm water (105-115° F)**
**½ cup sugar**
**½ teaspoon salt**
**1 egg, lightly beaten**
**½ cup vegetable shortening**
**3 cups all-purpose flour**
**1 tablespoon butter, melted and cooled**

In a small bowl, dissolve yeast in warm water; set aside for 5 minutes. Stir in sugar, salt, and egg. In a large mixing bowl, beat together shortening and yeast mixture until blended. Gradually add flour, 1 cup at a time; beat until flour is absorbed and dough holds together. Turn dough out onto a lightly floured surface. Roll to a ¼-inch thickness. Cut into rounds with a 3-inch cookie cutter. Arrange rounds on baking sheet. Brush with melted butter, fold in half, and pinch edges to seal. Cover lightly with a kitchen towel. Set aside to rise until rolls have doubled in bulk, about 45 minutes. Preheat oven to 350° F. Bake for 12 to 15 minutes. Immediately remove from pans; cool on a rack.

# Orange Yogurt Bread

Makes 1 loaf

**½ cup butter**
**1½ cups sugar**
**2 eggs**
**1½ cups all-purpose flour**
**1½ teaspoons baking powder**
**½ teaspoon salt**
**½ cup orange juice**
**1 tablespoon grated orange peel**
**1 cup unflavored yogurt**

Preheat oven to 350° F. Grease and flour a 9 x 5-inch loaf pan. In a large mixing bowl, cream butter and sugar until fluffy. Add eggs; beat well. In a separate bowl, stir together flour, baking powder, and salt. In a small bowl, combine orange juice, orange peel, and yogurt. Add dry ingredients to creamed mixture alternately with yogurt mixture. Pour batter into prepared pan. Bake for 55 minutes or until a wooden pick inserted near the center comes out clean. Cool in pan 10 minutes. Remove bread from pan and cool on a rack. Frost with Orange Icing while bread is still warm.

## Orange Icing

**¾ cup powdered sugar**
**4 tablespoons orange juice**
**1 tablespoon orange liqueur** *or* **Triple Sec**

In a small bowl, combine sugar, orange juice, and liqueur; beat until mixture is smooth.

# Orange Tea Bread

Makes 1 loaf

**1 cup orange marmalade**
**2 eggs**
**1 cup fresh orange juice**
**2 tablespoons butter, melted**
**2¾ cups all-purpose flour**
**½ cup sugar**
**2 teaspoons baking powder**
**1 teaspoon baking soda**
**¼ teaspoon salt**
**¾ cup chopped walnuts**
**2 teaspoons grated orange peel**
**1 teaspoon grated lemon peel**

Preheat oven to 350° F. Grease and flour a 9 x 5-inch loaf pan. In a mixing bowl, stir together marmalade, eggs, orange juice, and butter until blended. In a separate bowl, stir together flour, sugar, baking powder, soda, and salt. Add orange mixture; beat until smooth. Fold in nuts, orange peel, and lemon peel. Spoon batter into prepared pan; bake for 1 hour or until a wooden pick inserted near the center comes out clean. Cool in the pan for 10 minutes; turn out onto a rack to cool completely.

# Summer Fall Muffins

Makes 12 muffins

**2 cups all-purpose flour**
**½ cup granulated sugar**
**¼ cup firmly packed light brown sugar**
**1 tablespoon baking powder**
**1 teaspoon cinnamon**
**½ teaspoon salt**
**2 eggs**
**5 tablespoons vegetable oil**
**¾ cup milk**
**1½ cups dates *or* fresh cranberries**

Preheat oven to 375° F. Grease a 12-cup muffin pan. In a mixing bowl, combine flour, sugars, baking powder, cinnamon, and salt. In a separate bowl, beat eggs, oil, and milk until well blended. Add egg mixture to flour mixture; beat just until batter is moistened. Stir in dates. Fill muffin cups ⅔ full. Bake for about 20 minutes. Remove muffins from pan immediately; cool on a wire rack.

# Broiled Sourdough Slices

Makes 4 servings

**1/2 loaf sourdough French bread**
**1/2 cup butter *or* margarine, softened**
**2 to 3 cloves garlic, minced**
**1/4 cup minced fresh parsley**
**1/4 cup freshly grated Romano *or* Parmesan cheese**

Preheat broiler. Slice French bread. Blend remaining ingredients and spread evenly over bread slices. Broil until golden and bubbly.

# Panettone

Makes 1 loaf

**2 packages active dry yeast**
**1 tablespoon sugar**
**½ cup warm water (105-115° F)**
**3½ cups all-purpose flour**
**3 eggs**
**2 egg yolks**
**1 teaspoon vanilla**
**2 teaspoons grated lemon peel**
**2 teaspoons grated orange peel**
**¾ cup butter at room temperature**
**¾ cup dark raisins**
**¼ cup chopped candied orange peel**
**1 egg, lightly beaten**

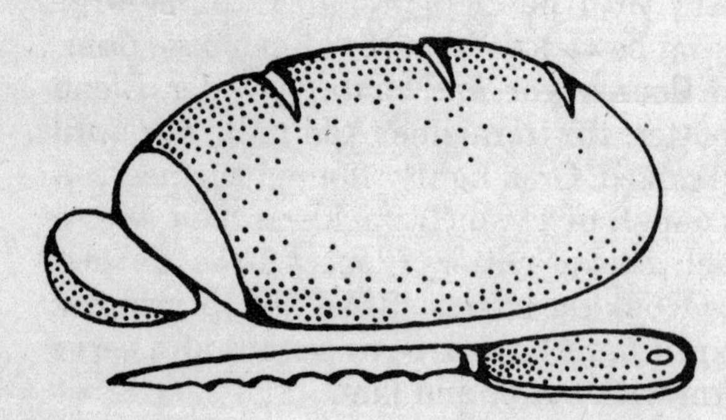

In a large mixing bowl, dissolve yeast with sugar in warm water; set aside for 5 minutes. Stir ½ cup of the flour into yeast; set aside in a warm place until doubled in volume. Beat in remaining flour, eggs, egg yolks, vanilla, and grated citrus peel. Turn dough out onto a lightly floured surface and knead until dough is soft and elastic, about 6 minutes. Gradually knead in butter. Knead in raisins and candied orange peel. Place dough in a lightly oiled bowl. Turn dough to oil top. Cover lightly with a towel and set aside until doubled in bulk, about 1½ hours.

Punch dough down and knead until smooth, about 5 minutes. Place in a greased 1-pound coffee can. Set aside until doubled in bulk, about 50 minutes. Brush top of dough with egg. Bake at 400° F for 10 minutes; reduce heat to 350° F and continue baking for 35 minutes or until golden brown. Cool 5 minutes in the can. Turn out onto a rack to cool completely.

# Soda Bread with Raisins

Makes 1 loaf

**3 cups all-purpose flour**
**¼ cup sugar**
**2 teaspoons baking powder**
**1 teaspoon baking soda**
**½ teaspoon salt**
**1 cup raisins**
**½ cup candied fruit, chopped**
**1¼ cups buttermilk**
**2 tablespoons vegetable oil**

Preheat oven to 375° F. Grease a baking sheet. In a bowl, stir together flour, sugar, baking powder, soda, and salt. Stir in raisins and candied fruit. In a mixing bowl, beat buttermilk with oil until blended. Stir in flour mixture; beat until a soft dough forms. Turn dough out onto a lightly floured surface. Knead for 1 minute. On prepared baking sheet, shape dough into a round loaf. Bake for 40 minutes.

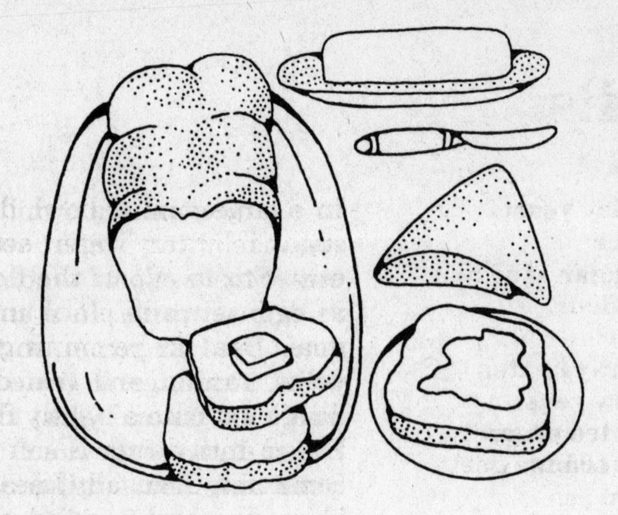

# English Scones

Makes 24 scones

**1½ cups all-purpose flour**
**1½ cups cake flour**
**4 tablespoons sugar**
**2 tablespoons baking powder**
**6 tablespoons butter at room temperature**
**½ cup raisins**
**1 cup milk**

Preheat oven to 400° F. Cover 2 baking sheets with parchment paper. In a large mixing bowl, stir together all-purpose flour, cake flour, sugar, and baking powder. Blend in butter; stir in raisins. Add milk; stir until well mixed. On a lightly floured surface, roll out dough to a ½-inch thickness. Cut with a 2-inch cookie cutter. Place scones on prepared baking sheets. Bake for 15 minutes or until light brown. Split scones and serve warm with butter and jam.

# Spoon Bread

Makes 8 servings

**1½ cups boiling water**
**1 cup cornmeal**
**1 tablespoon butter, melted**
**3 eggs, separated**
**1 cup buttermilk**
**1 teaspoon sugar**
**1 teaspoon baking powder**
**¼ teaspoon baking soda**
**½ teaspoon salt**
**Butter at room temperature**

Preheat oven to 375° F. Grease a 2-quart casserole. In a large bowl, stir boiling water into cornmeal. To prevent lumping, stir until the mixture is cool. Blend in butter and egg yolks. Stir in buttermilk, sugar, baking powder, soda, and salt. Beat egg whites just until soft peaks form; fold into batter. Pour batter into prepared casserole; bake 45 to 50 minutes. Spoon onto a plate. Serve with butter; eat with a fork or spoon.

# Pecan Rolls

Makes 1 dozen rolls

½ cup milk
4 tablespoons butter
⅓ cup granulated sugar
½ teaspoon salt
1 large egg at room temperature, lightly beaten
1 package active dry yeast
1 teaspoon granulated sugar
¼ cup warm water (105 to 115° F)
2½ to 3 cups all-purpose flour

3 tablespoons melted butter
1 teaspoon cinnamon
6 tablespoons granulated sugar
½ cup packed brown sugar
1 cup chopped pecans

In a saucepan, scald milk. Add the 4 tablespoons butter, sugar, and salt; stir until butter melts. Cool to room temperature. Stir in egg; set aside. In a small bowl, dissolve yeast and sugar in water. Set aside for about 5 minutes. In a mixing bowl, combine milk mixture and yeast mixture; blend well. Stir in 1 cup of the flour. Gradually work in remaining flour until dough holds together. Turn dough out onto a lightly floured surface. Knead until smooth. Place dough in a greased bowl; turn to grease top. Place in a warm, draft-free area to rise until doubled in bulk, about 1½ hours.

Preheat oven to 375° F. Turn dough out onto a lightly floured surface. Roll out to an 8 x 16-inch rectangle. Brush the top with melted butter. Sprinkle cinnamon and sugar evenly over dough. Roll up jelly roll style. Cut into 12 pieces. Generously grease a 12-cup muffin pan. Sprinkle brown sugar and pecans into the bottom of each cup. Top with round of dough. Cover and let rise for 30 minutes in a draft-free area. Bake for 15 minutes. Turn rolls out onto a baking rack to cool.

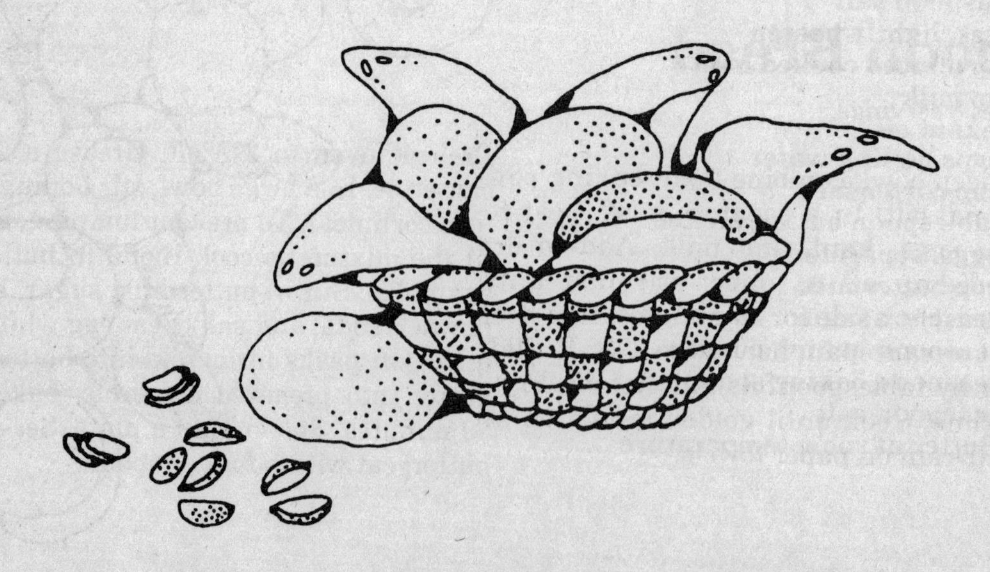

# Fresh Herb Scones

Makes 4 servings

- 2 cups all-purpose flour
- ½ cup whole wheat flour
- 1 to 2 teaspoons sugar substitute
- 2 teaspoons baking powder
- 1 teaspoon crushed rosemary
- 1 teaspoon baking soda
- 1 teaspoon salt
- 1 teaspoon thyme
- 1 teaspoon oregano
- ¼ cup butter *or* margarine
- 1 egg(reserve 1 tablespoon white)
- ½ cup plus 2 tablespoons buttermilk

Preheat oven to 400°. Combine or blend first 9 ingredients in bowl or food processor. Cut butter *or* margarine into small pieces and work into flour mixture with food processor or pastry blender until blended. In a separate bowl beat egg with buttermilk and stir into mixture. Turn dough out on a floured board and knead for 2 minutes. Shape into 2 thick circles, 5 inches in diameter. Cut each into quarters and place on lightly greased baking sheet with wedges about 1/2 inch apart. Brush with reserved egg white. Bake for 15 to 20 minutes or until nicely browned. Serve warm.

# Ham Fritters

Makes 6 to 8 servings

- 1 cup all-purpose flour
- 1 teaspoon baking powder
- ½ teaspoon salt
- 2 eggs, lightly beaten
- 1 cup minced cooked ham
- ¼ cup milk
- Peanut oil

In a deep bowl, combine flour, baking powder, and salt. In a separate bowl, beat together eggs, ham, and milk. Add to dry ingredients all at once; stir just until blended. Set aside for 20 minutes. In a deep skillet or saucepan, heat oil to 375° F. Slide batter by tablespoonfuls into hot oil. Fry 4 at a time. Cook until golden brown on all sides. Drain on paper towels.

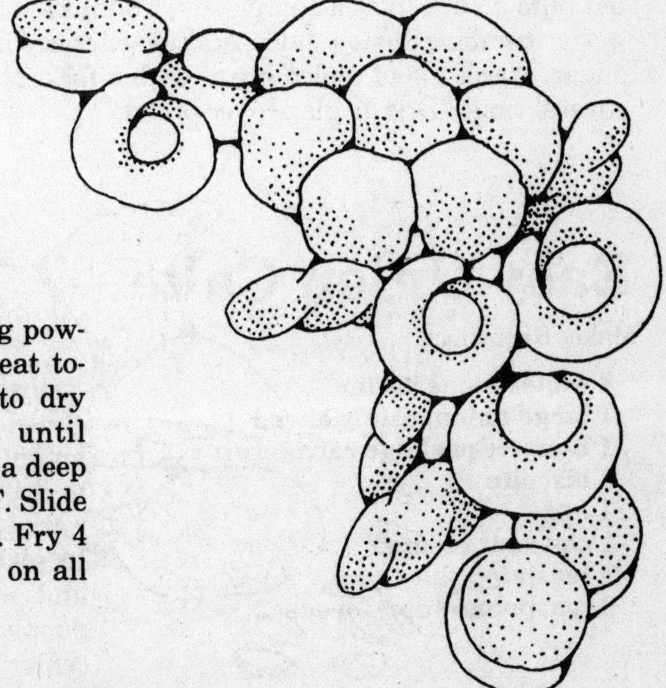

# Lemon Bread

Makes 1 loaf

**1 cup butter *or* margarine**
**2 cups sugar**
**4 eggs**
**3 cups all-purpose flour**
**½ teaspoon salt**
**½ teaspoon baking soda**
**1 cup buttermilk**
**Grated peel of 1 lemon**
**1 cup chopped walnuts**
**Juice from 3 lemons**
**1 cup powdered sugar**

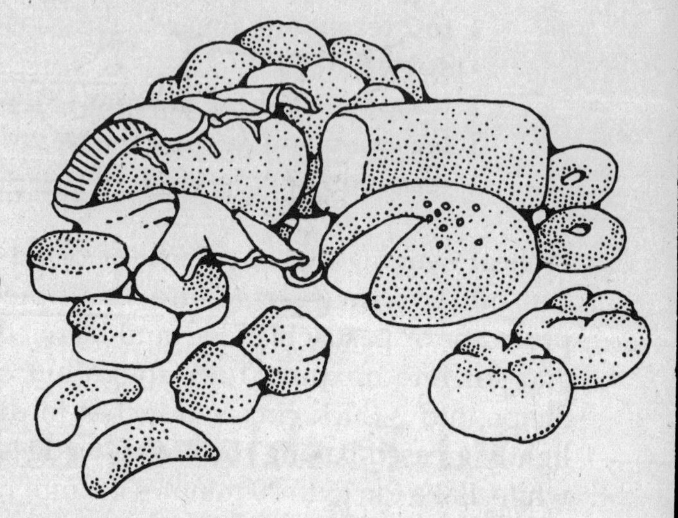

Preheat oven to 350° F. Grease and flour a 9 x 5-inch loaf pan. In a mixing bowl, cream butter and sugar. Add eggs, 1 at a time, beating well after each addition. In a separate bowl, stir together flour, salt, and soda. Add dry ingredients to creamed mixture alternately with buttermilk. Stir in lemon peel and walnuts. Pour batter into prepared pan. Bake for 1 hour or until a wooden pick inserted near the center comes out clean. Cool bread in pan 10 minutes; turn out onto a rack to cool completely. To make glaze, combine lemon juice and powdered sugar. Pierce top of cooled bread with a fork several times. Drizzle glaze over bread.

# Easy Onion Cake

Makes 8 servings

**4 tablespoons butter**
**1 large onion, thinly sliced**
**1 8-ounce package refrigerator biscuits**
**1 egg**
**1 cup sour cream**
**½ teaspoon salt**
**2 teaspoons poppy seeds**

Preheat oven to 375° F. In a large, heavy skillet over medium heat, melt butter. Add onion; sauté until tender. Arrange biscuits to cover the bottom of an ungreased 9-inch round cake pan. Spoon onion over biscuits. In a small bowl, beat egg with sour cream and salt; pour over onion. Sprinkle with poppy seeds. Bake for 30 minutes or until center is set.

# Desserts

## Old-Fashioned Bread Pudding

Makes 8 servings

**4½ cups crumbled stale rolls *or* bread**
**4 eggs**
**1½ cups sugar**
**2 teaspoons vanilla**
**1 teaspoon cinnamon**
**½ teaspoon nutmeg**
**¼ cup butter at room temperature**
**4 cups milk**
**½ cup golden raisins**
**1 teaspoon grated lemon peel**

Preheat oven to 350° F. Place crumbled bread on a cookie sheet; place in oven to crisp for about 10 minutes. Transfer to a 9 x 13-inch baking dish. In a mixing bowl, beat eggs and sugar until thick and lemon-colored. Add vanilla, cinnamon, and nutmeg; stir until blended. Beat in butter and milk. Sprinkle raisins and lemon peel over bread pieces. Pour egg mixture over all. Place pudding in a pan of warm water. Bake for 50 minutes or until a knife inserted in the center comes out clean. Cool slightly. Serve with Bourbon Sauce.

## Bourbon Sauce

**1 cup sugar**
**1 cup heavy cream**
**2 teaspoons butter**
**5 tablespoons water mixed with 1 teaspoon all-purpose flour**
**3 tablespoons bourbon**

In a small saucepan over medium heat, combine sugar, heavy cream, and butter. Bring to a boil, stirring constantly. Stir in flour-water mixture; cook until sauce thickens. Remove from heat and stir in bourbon.

# Blueberry Strawberry Buckle

Makes 9 servings

**½ cup butter *or* margarine at room temperature**
**1 cup sugar**
**1 egg**
**1 teaspoon vanilla**
**1½ cups all-purpose flour**
**1 teaspoon baking powder**
**1 teaspoon salt**
**½ cup milk**
**1 cup blueberries**
**1 cup sliced strawberries**
**½ teaspoon cinnamon**
**½ teaspoon nutmeg**
**Sweetened whipped cream *or* vanilla ice cream, optional**

Preheat oven to 350° F. Grease a 9-inch square baking pan. In a small bowl, cream ¼ cup of the butter and ½ cup of the sugar. Blend in egg and vanilla. In a small mixing bowl, stir together 1 cup of the flour, baking powder, and salt. Add dry ingredients to creamed mixture alternately with milk; stir until blended. Pour batter into prepared pan. Arrange fruit over batter. In a small bowl, combine remaining sugar, remaining flour, cinnamon, and nutmeg. Cut in remaining ¼ cup butter until mixture is crumbly. Sprinkle crumb mixture over fruit. Bake for 35 minutes. Serve with sweetened whipped cream or vanilla ice cream, if desired.

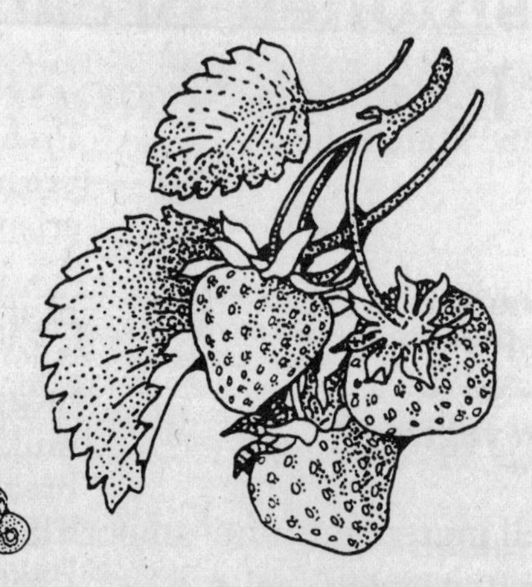

# Zabaglione

Makes 8 servings

**8 egg yolks**
**6 tablespoons sugar**
**¾ cup Marsala**
**1 pint fresh raspberries**

In a large, heatproof bowl, beat egg yolks until thick and lemon-colored. Gradually beat in sugar. Blend in wine. Place bowl over a pot of hot, but not boiling, water. Be sure bottom of the bowl does not touch water. Cook mixture, beating constantly, until mixture leaves sides of pan. Remove from heat. Divide berries among 8 sherbet glasses. Pour custard over berries. Serve warm.

# Rice Pudding

Makes 8 servings

- **1 quart milk**
- **¾ cup sugar**
- **4 eggs, beaten**
- **1 teaspoon vanilla**
- **2 cups cooked rice**
- **½ teaspoon cinnamon**
- **¼ teaspoon nutmeg**
- **¼ teaspoon salt**
- **1 cup golden raisins**
- **Light cream, optional**

**Preheat oven to 325° F. Butter a 2-quart baking dish. In a medium saucepan over medium heat, scald milk. Set aside to cool. In a separate bowl, beat sugar, eggs, and vanilla until well blended. Stir rice, spices, and salt into cooled milk. Stir egg mixture into rice mixture. Stir in raisins. Pour batter into prepared baking dish. Place baking dish in a large, shallow pan. Pour in hot water to a depth of 1 inch. Bake for 1 hour. Stir thoroughly. Bake an additional 30 minutes or until a knife inserted near the center comes out clean. Cool on a rack. Serve warm or cold in shallow bowls. Top with light cream, if desired.**

# Orange Papaya Smoothie

Makes 4 servings

- **1 ripe papaya, peeled, seeded, and chopped**
- **2 cups orange juice**
- **1 cup plain yogurt**
- **1 cup cracked ice**
- **1 banana, mashed**
- **1 teaspoon lime *or* lemon juice**

Purée or process all ingredients until smooth. Serve in tall glasses.

# Frozen Vanilla Custard

Makes 2 quarts

**6 eggs, lightly beaten**
**2 cups milk**
**¾ cup sugar**
**2 tablespoons honey**
**¼ teaspoon salt**
**2 cups heavy cream**
**1 tablespoon vanilla**

In a medium saucepan, beat eggs, milk, sugar, honey, and salt until well blended. Cook over low heat, stirring constantly, until the mixture thickens and coats a metal spoon. Cover and refrigerate until thoroughly chilled. Add heavy cream and vanilla; blend well. Pour mixture into a 1-gallon ice cream freezer can. Freeze according to manufacturer's directions.

# Prune Coffee Cake

Makes 1 loaf

**1½ cups pitted prunes**
**½ teaspoon cinnamon**
**¼ teaspoon nutmeg**
**1 teaspoon vanilla *or* 2 tablespoons Armagnac**
**2 cups all-purpose flour**
**1 teaspoon baking powder**
**1 teaspoon baking soda**
**½ teaspoon salt**
**½ cup shortening at room temperature**
**1 cup sugar**
**3 eggs, beaten**
**Grated peel of ½ orange**

Preheat oven to 325° F. Grease and flour a 9 x 5-inch loaf pan. In a small saucepan, combine prunes, 1 cup water, cinnamon, and nutmeg. Bring to a boil over medium heat. Reduce heat, cover, and simmer for 15 minutes. Drain prunes; reserve liquid. Add water to prune liquid to make ½ cup, if necessary. Stir vanilla into prune liquid; set aside. In a medium bowl, stir together flour, baking powder, soda, and salt. In a large mixing bowl, cream shortening and sugar. Add eggs to creamed mixture, 1 at a time, beating well after each addition. Add dry ingredients to creamed mixture alternately with prune liquid. Stir in prunes and orange peel. Pour batter into prepared pan. Bake 1½ hours. Cool in pan 10 minutes. Turn out onto a rack to cool completely.

# Spritz Cookies

Makes 5 to 6 dozen

**1 cup butter**
**¾ cup sugar**
**2 egg yolks**
**1 teaspoon almond extract**
**2 cups all-purpose flour**
**¼ teaspoon salt**

Preheat oven to 350° F. In a large bowl, cream butter and sugar. Blend in egg yolks and almond extract. In a separate bowl, stir together flour and salt; blend into creamed mixture. Fill a cookie press with the dough. Using a variety of discs, press onto an ungreased baking sheet. Decorate as desired. Bake for 8 to 10 minutes.

# Shortbread

Makes 16 servings

**2 cups butter at room temperature**
**1 cup sugar**
**4 cups all-purpose flour**
**1 cup semolina**
**Powdered sugar**

Preheat oven to 300° F. In a large mixing bowl, cream butter and sugar. Add half of the flour; stir to blend. Stir in remaining flour, 1 cup at a time. Add semolina; beat until dough holds together. Turn out onto a lightly floured surface; knead for 2 minutes. Divide dough into 4 parts. Pat each part into an 8-inch pie pan, pressing dough to even the surface. Prick the entire surface with a fork. Bake on the center shelf for 1¼ hours or until just beginning to turn golden brown. Cut into wedges while still warm. Sprinkle with powdered sugar. Store shortbread in airtight containers.

# English Raisin Almond Cake

Makes 8 servings

- ¾ cup butter
- ¾ cup sugar
- 4 eggs
- 2 cups all-purpose flour
- 1¼ teaspoons baking powder
- 1 tablespoon milk, optional
- 3 tablespoons ground almonds
- 1 cup dried currants
- 1 cup raisins
- ½ cup candied cherry halves
- ¼ cup chopped candied orange peel
- 2 teaspoons grated lemon peel
- ½ cup blanched split almonds

Preheat oven to 350° F. Butter and flour an 8-inch cake pan. In a large mixing bowl, cream butter and sugar. Add eggs, 1 at a time, beating well after each addition. In a separate bowl, stir together flour and baking powder. Add to egg mixture; blend well. If batter seems too dry, add 1 tablespoon milk. Stir in ground almonds, currants, raisins, cherries, orange peel, and lemon peel. Spoon batter evenly into prepared pan. Arrange almonds over top of cake in a decorative pattern. Bake for 1½ hours or until a wooden pick inserted near the center comes out clean. Cool 10 minutes in the pan; turn out onto a wire rack to cool completely. Wait 2 days before serving. This cake keeps well in an airtight container.

# Sour Cream Coffee Cake

Makes 8 servings

- 1 cup chopped walnuts
- ¾ cup sugar
- 1 teaspoon cinnamon
- ¼ cup butter
- 1 cup sugar
- 2 eggs, lightly beaten
- 1 cup sour cream
- 1 teaspoon vanilla
- 2 cups all-purpose flour
- 1 teaspoon baking powder
- 1 teaspoon baking soda
- ¼ teaspoon salt

Preheat oven to 350° F. Grease and flour a 9-inch springform pan.. In a small bowl, combine walnuts, ¾ cup sugar, and cinnamon; set aside. In a large bowl, cream butter and 1 cup sugar. Add eggs; beat until mixture is light and fluffy. Stir in sour cream and vanilla. In a separate bowl, stir together flour, baking powder, soda, and salt; blend into sour cream mixture. Pour half of the batter into prepared pan. Sprinkle half of the nut mixture over batter. Pour in remaining batter; sprinkle with remaining nut mixture. Bake for 35 minutes or until a wooden pick inserted near center comes out clean. Cool in pan on a rack.

# Rhubarb Kuchen

Makes 12 servings

**1¾ cups flour**
**1 teaspoon baking powder**
**2 tablespoons sugar**
**½ teaspoon salt**
**½ cup butter**
**¼ cup chopped nuts**
**2 egg yolks, lightly beaten**
**2 egg yolks**
**2 cups sugar**
**½ cup flour**
**4 to 5 cups rhubarb, cut in 1-inch pieces**
**Meringue**

In a bowl, stir together flour, baking powder, sugar, and salt. Cut in butter until mixture is crumbly. Stir in nuts and egg yolks until well mixed. Press into the bottom of a 9 x 12-inch baking pan.

Preheat oven to 350° F. In a separate bowl, beat egg yolks. Add sugar and flour; stir until blended. Stir in rhubarb. Pour rhubarb mixture into crust. Bake 45 minutes. Remove kuchen from oven. Reduce oven temperature to 325° F. Top kuchen with Meringue. Bake for 10 minutes or until Meringue is delicately browned.

## Meringue

**4 egg whites**
**¼ teaspoon salt**
**¼ teaspoon cream of tartar**
**¾ cup sugar**
**1 teaspoon vanilla**

In a deep bowl, beat egg whites until foamy. Add remaining ingredients; beat until stiff peaks form.

# Summer Fruit Pie

Makes 6 servings

**¾ cup crushed graham crackers**
**2 tablespoons melted margarine**
**1 teaspoon sugar**
**2 tablespoons apple jelly**
**1 tablespoon water**
**½ cup grapes**
**½ cup blueberries**
**½ cup strawberries, halved**
**2 fresh peaches, sliced**

Preheat oven to 350° F. In a bowl, stir together graham crackers, margarine, and sugar until well blended. Press crumb mixture into an 8-inch pie pan. Bake for 10 minutes. In a small saucepan, stir together jelly and water. Cook over low heat for 3 minutes. Arrange fruit over baked crust. Drizzle jelly mixture over fruit. Serve either chilled or at room temperature.

# Dips & Dressings

## Honey Dip with Fruit

Makes 1 cup

- 1 tablespoon honey
- 1/2 cup Neufchatel *or* ricotta cheese
- 1/2 cup plain yogurt
- Grated peel of 1/2 lime *or* 1/2 lemon
- Grated peel of 1/2 orange
- 1 tablespoon jam *or* preserves
- Choice of fruits

Combine all ingredients; mix well. Serve as a dip with your favorite fruits prepared in bite-size pieces.

## Crudités with Garlic Dip

Makes 4 servings

- 4 medium cloves garlic
- 2 large egg yolks, at room temperature
- 1/8 teaspoon salt
- 1/4 teaspoon Dijon-style mustard
- 3/4 cup olive oil
- 1 teaspoon lemon juice
- 1/2 teaspoon cold water
- 1 cup cauliflower florets, steamed
- 1 cup broccoli florets, steamed
- 4 green onions, trimmed
- 1/2 cup fresh mushrooms
- 4 carrots, cut into 3-inch sticks
- 4 stalks celery, cut into 3-inch sticks

Crush garlic and reduce to a paste; place in a blender or food processor. Add egg yolks, salt, and mustard; blend briefly. Gradually stir in half the oil. Add lemon and water; add the remaining oil; blend slowly and steadily. Transfer to a glass serving bowl; cover and refrigerate. To serve, place dip in the center of a large platter and arrange vegetables around it.

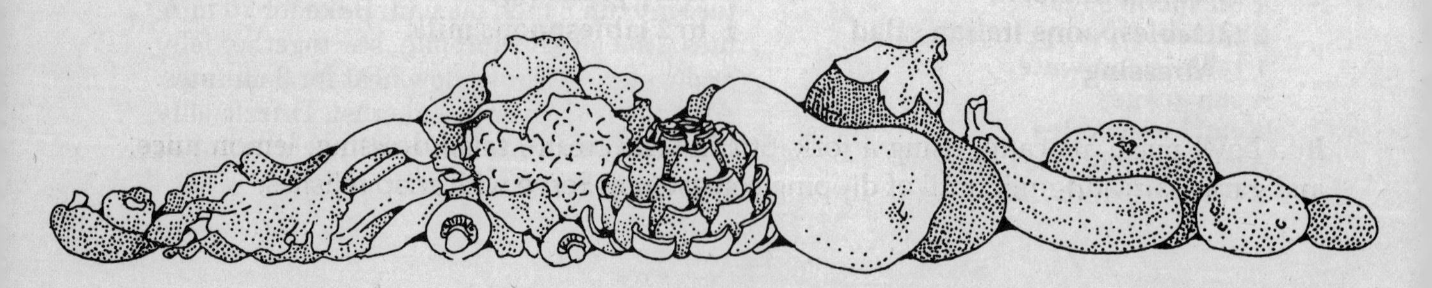

# Pesto Sauce

Makes 6 servings

1 cup fresh basil leaves
4 cloves garlic, minced
¼ cup pine nuts
¼ cup olive oil
½ cup grated Parmesan cheese
½ teaspoon salt

In a blender or a food processor, puree all ingredients until the consistency of a thick puree. Drizzle room temperature sauce over piping hot cooked pasta.

# Avocado Dip with Vegetables

Makes approximately 1 cup

1 avocado, peeled and seeded
⅓ cup sour cream
2 tablespoons Italian salad dressing
1 teaspoon lemon juice
Dash garlic salt
1 to 2 tablespoons milk

In a bowl mash avocado, using a fork. Stir in sour cream, salad dressing, lemon juice, and garlic salt; add milk until of dipping consistency. Serve with crisp relishes.

# Eggs

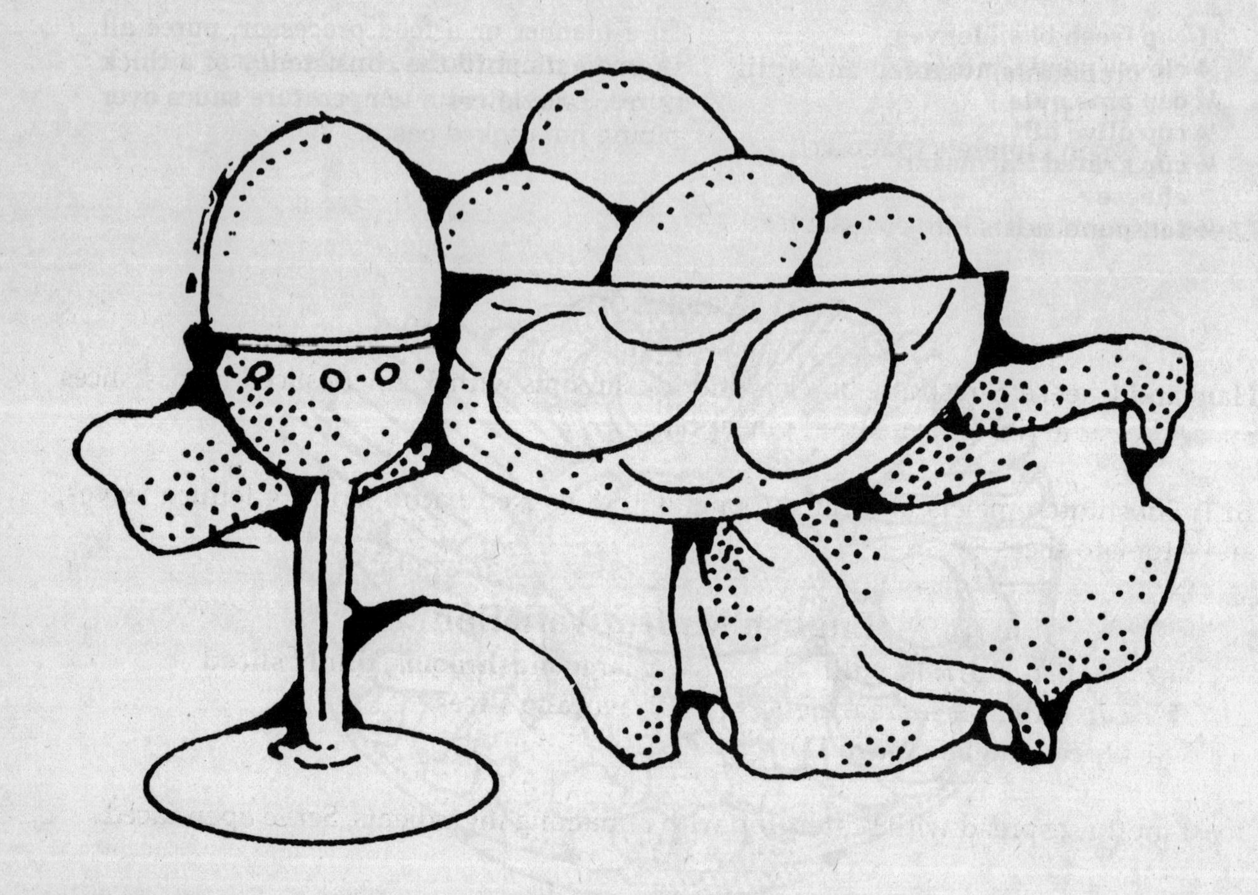

## Goldenrod Eggs

Makes 6 servings

**6 hard-boiled eggs**
**5 tablespoons butter**
**4 tablespoons all-purpose flour**
**½ teaspoon salt**
**¼ teaspoon white pepper**
**2 cups milk**
**6 slices bread**

Separate whites and yolks of eggs; set aside. In a saucepan over low heat, melt butter. Stir in flour, salt, and pepper. Gradually blend in milk. Cook over medium heat, stirring constantly, until mixture thickens. Slice egg whites into sauce. Toast bread and place on individual serving dishes. Pour sauce over toast. Crumble egg yolks on top of each serving.

# Breakfast Sandwiches

Makes 4 servings

**4 croissants, warmed and split in half**
**4 Open Omelets (page 11)**
**4 large mushrooms, thinly sliced**
**12 avocado slices**

Layer all ingredients into croissants.

## Variations

**Ham and Cheese:** Substitute omelets and mushrooms with 8 ounces sliced ham, 4 slices Swiss cheese, and 8 ounces sliced pineapple.

**BLT:** Substitute omelets and mushrooms with 8 cooked bacon strips, 4 lettuce leaves, and 4 tomato slices.

## English Muffin Variation

**2 English muffins, split**
**1/4 cup butter *or* margarine**
**4 Open Omelets (page 11)**
**4 large mushrooms, thinly sliced**
**12 avocado slices**

Toast muffins; spread with butter. Top with remaining ingredients. Serve open-faced.

# Chicken Timbales

Makes 6 servings

1½ cups chopped cooked chicken
¾ cup shredded Cheddar cheese
1½ cups milk
6 eggs, lightly beaten
2 tablespoons instant minced onion
½ teaspoon salt
½ teaspoon paprika
3 teaspoons grated Parmesan cheese

Preheat oven to 350° F. Place 6 custard cups in a baking pan. Measure ¼ cup chicken and 2 tablespoons Cheddar cheese into each cup. Heat milk until just below simmering; set aside. In a mixing bowl, beat together eggs, onion, salt, and paprika. Stir milk into egg mixture until well blended. Pour egg mixture into custard cups. Sprinkle each cup with ½ teaspoon Parmesan cheese. Place baking pan in oven. Pour water into pan to within ½ inch of the top of custard cups. Bake until knife inserted near center of the custard comes out clean, about 25 minutes. Remove custard cups from hot water. Gently loosen custards with a spatula; invert onto serving plates.

# Zucchini Frittata

Makes 4 servings

8 eggs
½ teaspoon seasoned salt
¼ teaspoon white pepper
4 tablespoons butter *or* margarine
3 cups zucchini coins, cut in fourths
½ cup finely chopped onion
⅓ cup grated Parmesan cheese
Parsley

In a medium bowl, beat eggs with salt and pepper; set aside. In a large skillet over medium heat, melt 3 tablespoons of the butter. Add zucchini and onion; sauté until vegetables are tender but not brown. Remove from skillet; set aside, covering to keep warm. In same skillet, melt remaining tablespoon butter. Pour eggs into skillet. Tilt pan while lifting edges of the omelet with a spatula so uncooked eggs can flow to bottom of pan. Cook over medium heat until bottom is golden and eggs are partially set, about 5 to 7 minutes. Sprinkle cheese over eggs. Top with zucchini-onion mixture. Cover and cook 3 minutes more. Garnish with parsley. Serve in wedges.

# Mushroom Quiche

Makes 6 servings

**2 tablespoons butter *or* margarine**
**½ pound mushrooms, sliced**
**¼ cup sliced green onions**
**1 baked 9-inch pie shell**
**1 cup shredded Swiss cheese**
**4 eggs**
**1 cup half-and-half *or* milk**
**¼ cup grated Parmesan cheese**
**½ teaspoon salt**
**½ teaspoon dry mustard**
**¼ teaspoon white pepper**

**Preheat oven to 375° F. In a large skillet over medium heat, melt butter. Add mushrooms and onions; sauté until mushrooms are tender. Arrange mushrooms and onions evenly in pie shell. Sprinkle with Swiss cheese. In a mixing bowl, beat together remaining ingredients until well blended. Pour into pie shell. Bake until a knife inserted near the center comes out clean, about 35 minutes. Let quiche stand 5 minutes before serving.**

# Mexican Breakfast

Makes 4 servings

**2 teaspoons safflower oil**
**1 small red onion, chopped**
**½ green pepper, seeded and diced**
**2 12-ounce jars salsa**
**8 eggs, lightly beaten**
**¼ cup sliced jalapeño peppers**
**1 tablespoon butter *or* margarine**
**4 large corn tortillas**
**½ cup grated medium Cheddar cheese**
**Sliced green onion**
**Sliced jalapeño peppers**
**Chopped fresh cilantro *or* parsley**

Heat oil in medium saucepan. Sauté onion and green pepper in oil. Add salsa and simmer, uncovered, about 10 minutes. Remove sauce from heat. In a bowl, mix eggs and jalapeños. In a large skillet melt butter *or* margarine over medium heat. Scramble egg mixture in butter *or* margarine until eggs are cooked but still moist.

Dip tortillas in salsa mixture until soft. Spoon ¼ of the scrambled eggs down center of each tortilla; roll up and place enchilada, seam side down, in a casserole dish. Repeat with each tortilla. Reheat remaining sauce to boiling. Pour evenly over enchiladas and sprinkle with cheese. Place under broiler, 4 inches from heat source, until cheese melts. Garnish with onion, jalapeños, and cilantro.

# Lunch in a Skillet

Makes 6 servings

- 3 to 4 slices bacon, diced
- 1 cup frozen Southern-style hash brown potatoes
- ¼ cup chopped onion
- 6 eggs
- ⅓ cup water
- ½ teaspoon salt
- ½ teaspoon dill

In a large skillet over medium heat, cook bacon until crisp. Transfer to paper towels to drain. Pour off all but 3 tablespoons drippings. Add potatoes and onion. Cook, stirring occasionally, until potatoes begin to brown, about 5 minutes. Beat eggs with water, salt, and dill; stir in bacon. Pour over potato mixture in skillet. Cook, stirring occasionally, until eggs are cooked through but still moist.

# Crustless Carrot Quiche

Makes 6 servings

- 2 cups finely shredded carrots
- 6 eggs
- 1¼ cups milk
- 1 tablespoon instant minced onion
- ½ teaspoon salt
- ¼ teaspoon ground ginger
- ⅛ teaspoon white pepper
- 1 cup shredded Cheddar cheese

Preheat oven to 350° F. Butter a 9-inch quiche pan. Place carrots in a saucepan with just enough water to cover. Simmer, covered, until carrots are tender, about 5 minutes. Drain thoroughly. In a separate bowl, beat eggs with milk, onion, salt, ginger, and pepper. Stir in carrots and cheese. Pour batter into prepared pan. Place pan in a shallow pan of hot water. Bake for about 35 minutes or until a knife inserted near the center comes out clean. Let quiche stand for 5 minutes before serving.

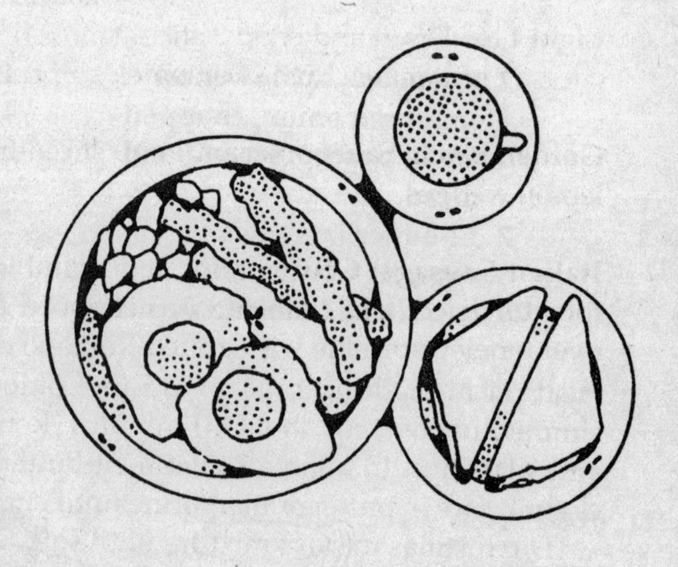

# Open Omelet Variations

Makes 4 servings

**4 eggs, separated**
**1/4 teaspoon salt**
**1/4 teaspoon cream of tartar**
**2 tablespoons water**
**1 to 2 teaspoon butter *or* margarine**
**1/2 to 1 cup topping of your choice**

Preheat oven to 350°. Beat egg whites with salt and cream of tartar at high speed until stiff but not dry. Beat yolks with water at high speed until thick and lemon-colored, about 5 minutes. Fold yolks into whites.

Heat butter *or* margarine in 10-inch omelet pan over medium heat until just hot enough to sizzle a drop of water. Pour in omelet mixture and carefully smooth the surface. Cook until puffy and lightly browned on the bottom, about 5 minutes.

Bake in oven for about 10 minutes or until knife inserted in the center comes out clean. Cover surface with chosen topping. Cut in half or in wedges to serve. Garnish as desired.

## Omelet Toppings

**Light Lox:** Drain and chop 2 slices smoked salmon. Combine with 4 ounces Neufchatel cheese until mixed. Spread on omelet. Sprinkle with lemon juice and chopped chives.

**Garden Patch:** Sauté or steam 1 cup sliced fresh vegetables of your choice. Garnish with lemon wedges.

**Italian Sausage:** Cook, drain, and crumble 2 Italian sausages. Combine with 1 large tomato, diced, and 2 tablespoons chopped fresh basil *or* 1 tablespoon dried basil. Ladle over omelet; sprinkle with grated Romano cheese.

# Spicy Scrambled Egg Pastries

Makes 4 servings

- 1 tablespoon vegetable oil
- 1/3 cup julienne cut green pepper
- 1/3 cup julienne cut red pepper
- 2 to 3 tablespoons minced onion
- 1 clove garlic, minced
- 1/3 cup salsa
- 1/4 cup finely chopped ham
- 10 eggs, beaten
- 8 puff pastry shells, baked according to package directions
- Salsa

In a medium skillet heat oil and sauté green and red peppers for 1 minute. Add onion and garlic and continue sautéing until onion becomes transparent and soft. Add salsa and ham; cook 5 minutes. Stir in eggs and scramble until firm but still moist. Serve eggs in puff pastry shells and garnish with extra salsa to taste.

# Cottage Cheese Omelet

Makes 1 serving

- ½ cup cottage cheese
- 1 tablespoon chopped chives
- 2 eggs
- 2 tablespoons water
- ¼ teaspoon basil
- ¼ teaspoon pepper
- 1 tablespoon butter

In a small bowl, combine cottage cheese and chives; set aside. Beat eggs with water, basil, and pepper. In an 8-inch omelet pan or skillet, heat butter until it sizzles. Pour egg mixture into skillet. Tilt pan while lifting edges of omelet so uncooked eggs can flow underneath. While top is still moist and creamy, spoon cottage cheese onto half of the omelet. Fold omelet over filling.

# Chived Cheese Omelet

Makes 2 servings

- 4 eggs
- ¼ cup water
- 1 tablespoons chopped chives
- ¼ teaspoon salt
- Dash white pepper
- 1½ tablespoons butter
- ½ cup shredded Cheddar cheese
- Chive flowers

In a mixing bowl, beat eggs with water, chives, salt, and pepper. In a 10-inch skillet, heat butter until it begins to sizzle. Pour in egg mixture. When edges set, tilt pan while lifting edges of omelet so that uncooked eggs flow to bottom of pan. While top of omelet is still moist and creamy, sprinkle ¼ cup of the cheese over half of the omelet. Fold omelet over cheese; turn out onto a platter. Top with remaining cheese. Garnish with chive flowers, if available.

# Ham and Green Pepper Soufflé

Makes 6 servings

- ¼ cup butter *or* margarine
- ¼ cup all-purpose flour
- ½ teaspoon salt
- 1 cup milk
- 1 cup minced cooked ham
- 1 small green pepper, chopped
- 4 eggs, separated
- ½ teaspoon cream of tartar

Preheat oven to 350° F. Butter and flour a 1½-quart soufflé dish or casserole. In a medium saucepan over medium heat, melt butter. Blend in flour and salt. Add milk all at once. Cook, stirring constantly, until mixture thickens and bubbles. Stir in ham and green pepper. Remove sauce from heat. Lightly beat egg yolks; add to sauce. Wash the beaters. In a large bowl, beat egg whites with cream of tartar until stiff peaks form. Pour sauce mixture over egg whites; fold together just until blended. Pour into prepared dish. For a "top hat," draw a circle about 1½ inches from the edge of dish with the tip of a spoon inserted 1 inch deep. Bake for 35 minutes or until a knife inserted between the center and edge of soufflé comes out clean. Serve immediately.

# Fruit Omelet

Makes 2 omelets

**½ cup flaked coconut**
**1 banana, sliced**
**4 eggs**
**½ cup water**
**½ teaspoon salt**
**¼ teaspoon white pepper**
**3 tablespoons butter**

Gently mix flaked coconut with banana; set aside. In a mixing bowl, beat together eggs, water, salt, and pepper. Heat half of the butter in a 10-inch omelet pan or skillet until butter sizzles. Pour in half of the egg mixture. Tilt pan while lifting edges of omelet with a spatula so that uncooked egg flows to the bottom of the pan. While top of omelet is still moist and creamy, spread ¼ cup of the banana filling on half of the omelet. With a pancake turner, fold omelet over filling. Top with ¼ cup of the filling. Sprinkle with powdered sugar. Repeat with remaining ingredients.

# California Omelet

Makes 1 serving

**7 fresh snow peas**
**½ red bell pepper, thinly sliced**
**1 tablespoon butter**
**3 ounces small raw shrimp, peeled and deveined**
**3 eggs, lightly beaten**
**1 teaspoon parsley**
**Salt and pepper to taste**
**Dill sprigs**

In a small saucepan, bring 1 cup salted water to a boil. Add snow peas; boil 1 minute. Add red pepper; boil 2 more minutes. Drain and immediately rinse with cold water; set aside. In a 6-inch skillet over medium heat, melt butter. Add shrimp; sauté until shrimp are opaque, about 4 minutes. Add beaten eggs. Cook, stirring constantly, until eggs just begin to set. Add snow peas, pepper, and parsley; cook and stir until eggs are almost set. Cook without stirring for 1 minute more or until bottom is set. Season to taste; garnish with dill sprigs.

# Mushroom Filled Puffy Omelet

Makes 2 servings

**4 eggs, separated**
**¼ cup water**
**½ teaspoon cream of tartar** *or* **lemon juice**
**¼ teaspoon salt**
**1 tablespoon butter**
**Sour cream**

Preheat oven to 350° F. In a large mixing bowl, beat egg whites with water and cream of tartar just until stiff peaks form. In a small bowl, beat egg yolks with salt until thick and lemon-colored. Gently fold yolks into whites until thoroughly blended. In a 10-inch omelet pan or skillet with an oven-proof handle, heat butter over medium heat until it sizzles. Add eggs; gently smooth surface. Cook until puffed and lightly browned on bottom, about 5 minutes. Bake for 10 minutes or until a knife inserted near the center comes out clean. Loosen edges with a spatula. With a sharp knife, leaving bottom of omelet intact, cut along the diameter of omelet. Spoon filling over half of the omelet. Fold omelet over filling. Garnish filled omelet with a dollop of sour cream.

## Mushroom and Sour Cream Filling

**1 tablespoon butter**
**½ cup sliced fresh mushrooms**
**¼ cup sour cream**
**¼ teaspoon dillweed**

In a medium skillet over medium heat, melt butter. Add mushrooms; sauté until tender. Stir in sour cream and dillweed. Spoon into omelet.

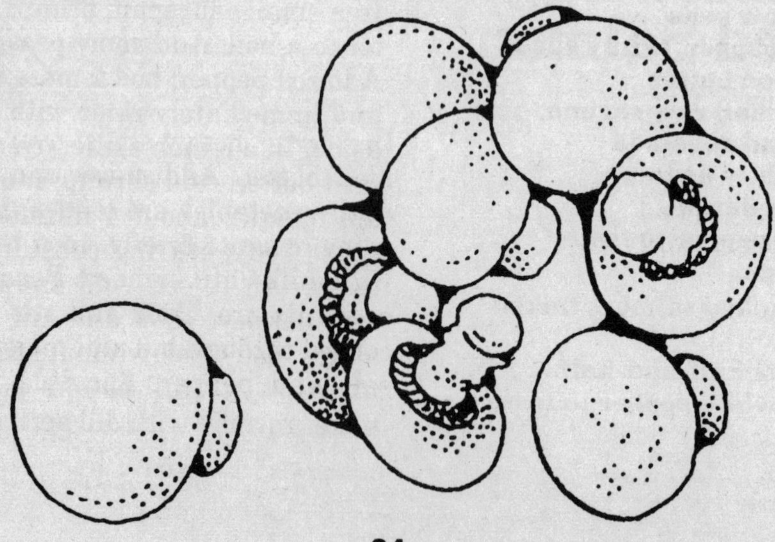

# Eggs Benedict

Makes 8 servings

**8 slices Canadian bacon**
**8 eggs**
**4 English muffins**
**Hollandaise Sauce**
**Orange slices**
**Fresh parsley**

Sauté Canadian bacon. Poach eggs. Split and toast English muffins. Top each muffin half with a slice of Canadian bacon. Place a poached egg on top of bacon. Spoon Hollandaise Sauce generously over egg. Garnish with orange slices and fresh parsley sprigs.

# Hollandaise Sauce

**6 egg yolks**
**1 tablespoon water**
**1½ teaspoons fresh lemon juice**
**1 cup butter**
**Salt to taste**

In the top of a double boiler over simmering water, place egg yolks and water. Beat until well blended and lemon-colored. Stir in lemon juice. Beat in the butter, a few pieces at a time. Beat until sauce is smooth. Stir in salt. Serve at once.

# Scrambled Eggs with Smoked Salmon

Makes 6 servings

**5 tablespoons butter** *or* **margarine**
**1 onion, thinly sliced**
**1 green pepper, thinly sliced**
**¼ pound smoked salmon, flaked**
**6 eggs**
**¼ cup milk** *or* **half-and-half**
**Salt and white pepper to taste**
**Parsley**

In a large, heavy skillet over medium heat, melt butter. Add onion and pepper; sauté until vegetables are tender. Stir in smoked salmon; sauté briefly. In a bowl, beat eggs with milk until blended. Pour eggs over salmon mixture. Cook and stir until eggs are cooked through but still moist. Season with salt and pepper. Sprinkle with parsley.

# Asparagus Soufflé

Makes 4 servings

Grated Parmesan cheese
1 10¾-ounce can condensed cream of asparagus soup
¾ cup shredded Cheddar cheese
4 eggs, separated
¼ teaspoon grated lemon peel

Preheat oven to 350° F. Butter a 1½-quart soufflé dish; dust with grated Parmesan cheese. Wrap a 4-inch band of triple-thickness aluminum foil around the dish, overlapping 2 inches. Fasten to soufflé dish so that collar extends 2 inches above rim of dish. Lightly butter 1 side of foil band; dust with Parmesan cheese. In a saucepan over medium heat, combine soup and Cheddar cheese. Cook and stir soup mixture until cheese melts. Remove from heat; add gradually to unbeaten egg yolks. Beat until mixture is well blended. With clean beaters, beat egg whites until stiff peaks form. Fold in lemon peel. Gently fold soup mixture into egg whites. Pour into soufflé dish. Bake for 45 minutes or until soufflé is puffy and delicately browned. Carefully remove foil band. Serve immediately.

# Deviled Eggs with Anchovies

Makes 6 servings

6 hard-boiled eggs
⅓ cup mayonnaise
4 tablespoons chopped fresh parsley
1 teaspoon anchovy paste
½ teaspoon salt
½ teaspoon cayenne
1 2½-ounce can anchovy fillets

Cut eggs in half lengthwise. Place yolks in a mixing bowl. Add mayonnaise, parsley, anchovy paste, salt, and cayenne; blend well. Mound mixture into egg whites. Place 1 anchovy fillet over each deviled egg. Refrigerate until ready to serve.

# Classic Quiche Lorraine

Makes 6 servings

**8 slices bacon, crisp-cooked and crumbled**
**1 cup shredded Swiss cheese**
**1 baked 9-inch pie shell**
**6 eggs**
**1¼ cups half-and-half *or* milk**
**½ teaspoon salt**
**¼ teaspoon nutmeg**
**¼ teaspoon white pepper**

Preheat oven to 375° F. Sprinkle bacon and cheese into pie shell. In a mixing bowl, beat together eggs, half-and-half, and seasonings until well blended. Pour over bacon and cheese. Bake for about 40 minutes or until a knife inserted near the center comes out clean. Let stand 5 minutes before serving.

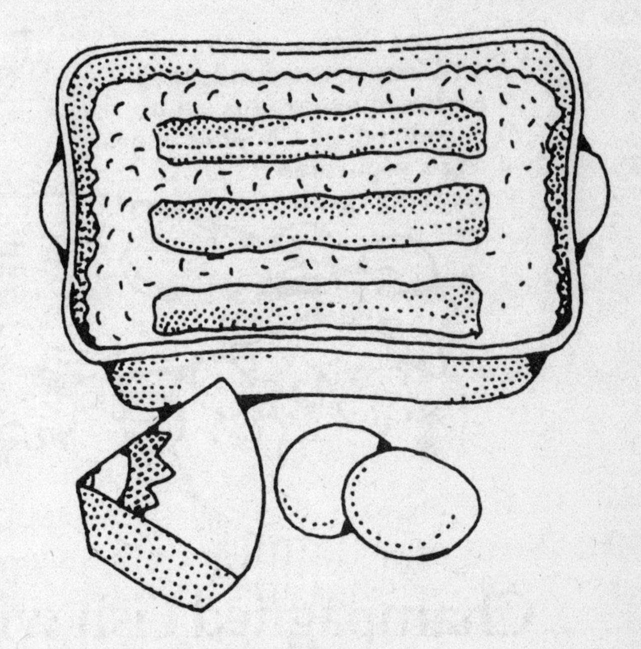

# Scrambled Eggs with Mushrooms

Makes 6 servings

**6 eggs**
**¼ cup milk *or* half-and-half**
**1 tablespoon chopped fresh basil**
**Salt and pepper to taste**
**3 tablespoons butter**
**2 tablespoons bacon drippings**
**½ pound mushrooms, sliced**
**4 slices bacon, crisp-cooked and crumbled**

In a small bowl, beat together eggs, milk, basil, salt, and pepper; set aside. In a large, heavy skillet over medium heat, heat butter and 2 tablespoons bacon drippings. Add mushrooms; sauté until tender. Stir in bacon. Pour eggs over mushrooms and bacon. Cook and stir until eggs are cooked through but still moist.

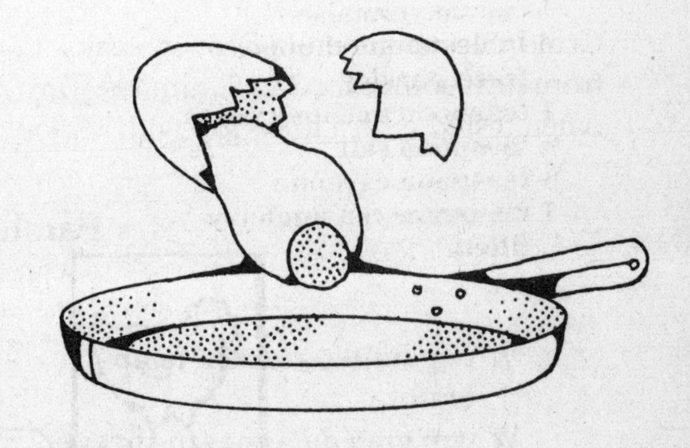

# Fish & Seafood

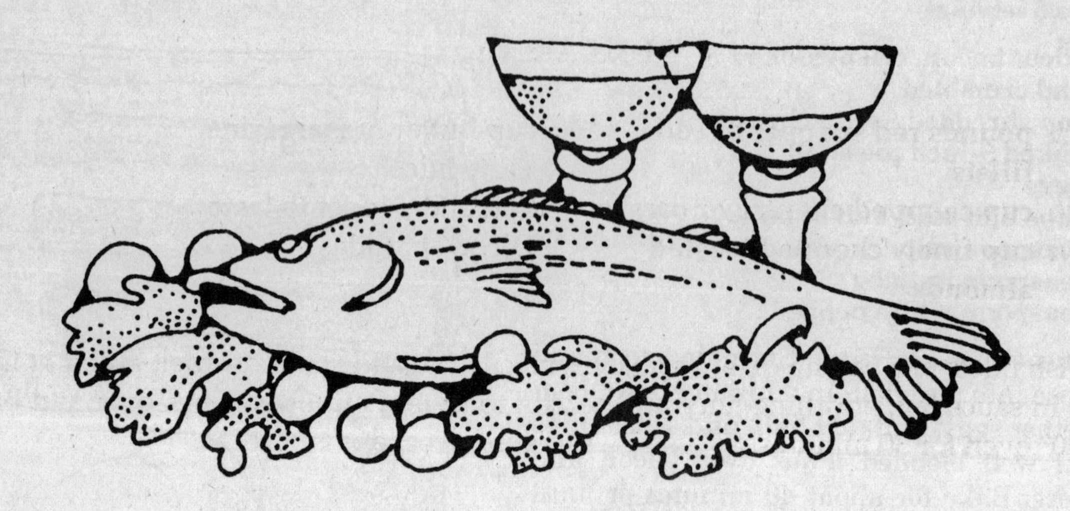

## Champagned Fish with Parsley Butter

Makes 4 servings

**Freshly ground pepper**
**4 1¼-pound fish steaks, cut 1 inch thick (halibut, swordfish, *or* salmon)**
**½ cup champagne**
**Parsley Butter (below)**

Grind pepper generously over steaks. Pour champagne evenly over fish. Broil 4 inches from heat source for 3 to 5 minutes. Turn. Broil 4 minutes more or until fish flakes easily when tested with a fork. Top with a spoonful of Parsley Butter.

### Parsley Butter

Makes ¾ cup

**½ cup butter, at room temperature**
**¼ cup grated Parmesan cheese**
**½ cup chopped fresh parsley**
**1 to 2 cloves garlic, minced**

Combine all ingredients; blend well. Serve as directed.

# Mexican Snapper

Makes 4 servings

**1½ pounds red snapper or cod fillets**
**½ cup chopped cilantro *or* parsley**
**½ cup finely chopped toasted almonds**
**¼ cup butter *or* margarine**
**Lime juice**
**Salt and pepper to taste**
**Diced avocados**

Place fish fillets in a baking dish. Sprinkle with cilantro and almonds. Melt butter *or* margarine in saucepan; add lime juice and season to taste. Pour over fish. Cover and bake in a 350° oven for 30 minutes. Sprinkle with diced avocados and serve.

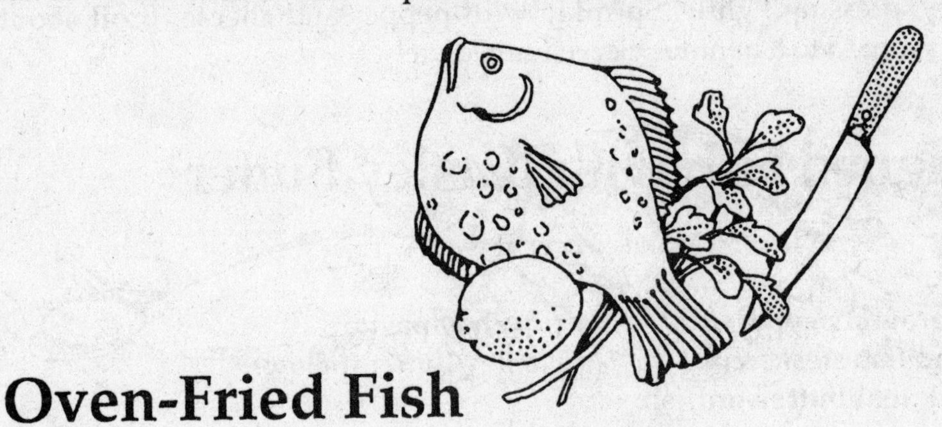

# Oven-Fried Fish

Makes 4 servings

**1 pound fresh fish fillets, thawed, cut ½-inch thick**
**1 beaten egg**
**2 tablespoons milk**
**¼ cup fine dry seasoned bread crumbs**
**2 tablespoons yellow cornmeal**
**2 tablespoons all-purpose flour**
**¼ teaspoon seasoned salt**
**6 tablespoons butter *or* margarine, melted**
**Lemon wedges**

Rinse fish and pat dry. In a shallow dish combine egg and milk. In a second shallow dish combine crumbs, cornmeal, flour, and salt. Dip fish in egg mixture, then in crumb mixture. Place in a shallow baking pan. Drizzle fish with melted butter. Bake at 500° for 4 to 6 minutes or until fish flakes easily when tested with a fork. Serve with lemon wedges.

# Crab-Stuffed Mushrooms

Makes 4 servings

3 tablespoons butter *or* margarine
12 large mushroom caps
2 cloves garlic, minced
½ cup monterey Jack *or* mozzarella cheese, shredded
1 6-ounce can flaked crabmeat
2 tablespoons red *or* white wine
1 to 2 teaspoons Worcestershire sauce
2 tablespoons fine dry bread crumbs
Freshly ground pepper
Shredded Monterey Jack cheese

Melt 1 tablespoon butter *or* margarine in sauté pan. Sauté mushroom caps, coating well with butter. Combine remaining butter *or* margarine and next 6 ingredients until blended. Place mushrooms on rimmed baking sheet. Evenly mound filling into each mushroom cavity, pressing lightly. Sprinkle with pepper and cheese. Broil about 6 inches from heat source 5 to 8 minutes. Serve immediately.

# Smoked Salmon á la Russe

Makes 4 servings

1 thin loaf French bread, sliced
Sour cream
2 4-ounce packages smoked salmon, thinly sliced
4 ounces caviar
Butter lettuce cups
Capers
Tomato wedges
Lemon twists

Spread bread slices with sour cream. Shape salmon slices into coronets; spoon a little caviar into each coronet. Place coronets on bread slices and arrange on lettuce cups. Garnish with remaining ingredients.

# Barbecued Shrimp

Makes 6 servings

**24 large shrimp, shelled, deveined, tails intact**
**1 large onion, thinly sliced**
**24 slices bacon**
**2 tablespoons brown sugar**
**2 tablespoons soy sauce**
**2 tablespoons dry sherry**
**3 cloves garlic, minced**
**½ teaspoon chili powder**
**½ teaspoon ground ginger**
**½ teaspoon salt**
**Shredded lettuce**

Cut shrimp along inside curve and open out butterfly-style. Place an onion on one half of shrimp; fold shrimp together. Wrap a slice of bacon around shrimp; secure with a toothpick. Set aside. Repeat with remaining shrimp. In a small bowl, mix brown sugar, soy sauce, sherry, garlic, and seasonings until well blended. Dip shrimp into marinade; set aside on a barbecue rack or broiling tray for 30 minutes. Barbecue over medium fire or grill under broiler until shrimp are cooked and bacon is crisp, about 5 minutes. Serve on a bed of shredded lettuce.

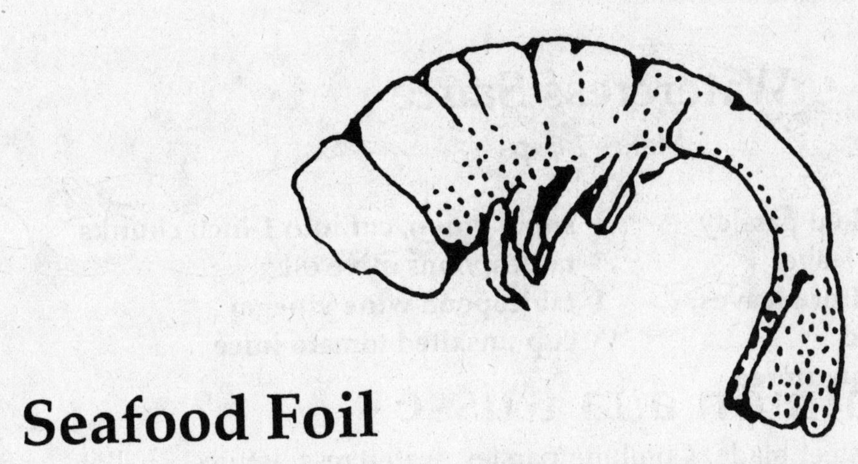

# Seafood Foil

Makes 4 servings

**4 1- to 1½-pound fish fillets (snapper, cod, *or* orange roughy)**
**½ cup thick salsa**
**8 large shrimp**
**Cilantro sprigs *or* parsley**
**1 lime, cut into wedges**

Cut foil into 8 heart-shaped pieces 1 inch longer than fillets. Place a fillet on each heart; top with 2 tablespoons salsa, 2 shrimp, and 2 sprigs of cilantro. Cover with another foil heart; seal edges. Bake at 400° for 10 to 12 minutes. Transfer to dinner plates. Cut a large "X" in each foil packet; turn back foil to expose fish. Garnish with lime wedges and serve steaming hot.

# Broiled Salmon with Linguine and Watercress Sauce

Makes 4 servings

- 4 salmon steaks, 3/4 inch thick
- 1 tablespoon chopped fresh marjoram *or* 1 teaspoon dried marjoram
- Salt and pepper to taste
- Watercress Sauce(next page)
- 4 ounces thin linguine, cooked and well drained

Sprinkle both sides of fish with marjoram and salt and pepper to taste. On an oiled rack 4 inches from heat source broil steaks until first side is lightly browned, 5 to 8 minutes. Turn and broil 5 to 8 minutes more, until fish flakes easily when tested with a fork. Combine 3/4 cup of Watercress Sauce with prepared linguine. Serve balance of the Watercress Sauce over the salmon steaks.

## Watercress Sauce

Makes 2 cups

- 1 cup tightly packed parsley
- 1 cup watercress leaves
- 6 large Boston lettuce leaves, centers removed
- 3 large shallots, quartered
- 1 small onion, cut into 1-inch chunks
- 3 tablespoons olive oil
- 1 tablespoon wine vinegar
- 1/3 cup unsalted tomato juice

Fit food processor with steel blade. Combine parsley, watercress, lettuce, shallots, and onions in work bowl; process with 3 on/off turns. Scrape down sides of bowl. Pour olive oil over mixture in a circular motion. Sprinkle with vinegar. Purée for 5 seconds. While machine is running, pour tomato juice through feed tube until well blended. Serve with salmon and linguine as directed.

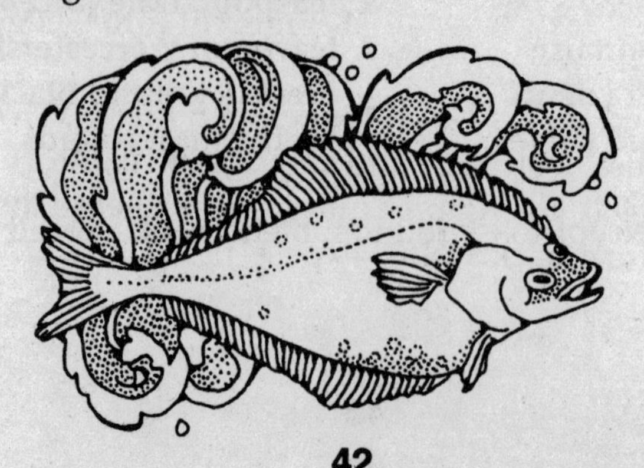

# Grilled Fish with Beurre Blanc Sauce

Makes 8 servings

3 tablespoons vegetable oil
1 3½-pound trout *or* salmon, cleaned, with head and tail intact
2 tablespoons wine vinegar
¼ cup white wine
1 medium onion, minced
½ cup butter

Place fish in an oiled wire broiling basket. Drizzle vegetable oil over fish. Cook on a hot grill about 5 inches from coals, turning after 5 minutes. Cook until fish flakes easily with a fork, about 10 more minutes. While fish cooks, prepare sauce. In a medium saucepan over medium heat, bring vinegar, wine, and onion to a boil. Simmer until mixture is reduced by half. Gradually blend in butter. Place fish on a serving platter; drizzle with sauce.

# Crabmeat Canapés

Makes 4 servings

1 4-ounce can crabmeat, well drained
2 tablespoon mayonnaise
2 tablespoons plain yogurt
1 tablespoon minced chives
1 tablespoon parsley
1 teaspoon lime juice
1 teaspoon Worcestershire sauce
Freshly ground black pepper to taste
Melba toast rounds

Combine all ingredients except toast rounds; blend well. Spread on toast rounds and serve immediately.

# Broiled Swordfish

Makes 4 servings

Freshly ground pepper
4 $1^3/_4$-pound swordfish *or* halibut steaks, cut 1 inch thick
1 tablespoon butter
1 large red pepper, cut into julienne strips
1 large green pepper, cut into julienne strips
4 tablespoons lemon juice
$^1/_4$ cup grated Parmesan cheese
2 tablespoons chopped fresh basil, optional
Lemon wedges

Preheat broiler to high. Grind pepper generously over swordfish. Heat butter over medium-high heat; add peppers and sauté until tender and well browned, about 10 minutes. Set aside. Broil swordfish 4 to 5 inches from heat source for 3 minutes. Sprinkle 2 tablespoons of lemon juice evenly over steaks. Turn fish, sprinkle remaining juice and broil for 5 minutes more or until fish flakes easily when tested with a fork. Spread peppers evenly over swordfish; sprinkle with Parmesan cheese and basil. Garnish with lemon wedges.

# Broiled Shrimp Kebabs

Makes 4 servings

**1 pound fresh large shrimp in shells**
**1/4 cup safflower oil**
**4 lemon slices**
**4 whole allspice**
**3 cloves garlic, minced**
**1 teaspoon crushed dried tarragon**
**1 teaspoon crushed dried oregano**
**Bay leaves, optional**

Peel and devein shrimp, leaving tail intact. In a shallow dish combine oil, lemon, allspice, garlic, tarragon, and oregano. Add shrimp. Cover and marinate for 1 hour at room temperature, stirring occasionally. Preheat broiler. Drain shrimp, reserving marinade; discard lemon and allspice. Thread shrimp on short skewers alternately with bay leaves, if desired. Place on unheated rack of broiler pan. Broil 4 inches from heat source for 3 to 4 minutes or until shrimp turn pink. Turn and brush occasionally with reserved marinade.

# Fried Kippers

Makes 8 servings

- 6 tablespoons butter
- 1 large onion, thinly sliced
- 8 smoked kippers

In a large, heavy skillet, heat butter. Add onion; sauté over medium heat until tender. Add 4 kippers; fry 4 minutes on each side, turning once. Repeat with remaining kippers, adding more butter as necessary. Serve warm with onions and pan juices.

# Fried Catfish

Makes 6 to 8 servings

- 2 pounds catfish fillets
- Salt and pepper to taste
- ½ teaspoon garlic powder
- Tabasco sauce
- 1 cup yellow cornmeal
- 3 tablespoons all-purpose flour
- Vegetable oil
- Tomato sauce *or* tartar sauce

Season fillets with salt, pepper, garlic powder, and Tabasco sauce. Cut fillets into 2-inch-wide strips. In a shallow bowl, stir together cornmeal and flour. Dredge fish in cornmeal mixture. Fill a heavy skillet with oil to a depth of 1 inch. Heat oil to 375° F. Fry fish, 4 pieces at a time, until cooked and golden brown. Serve with tomato sauce or tartar sauce.

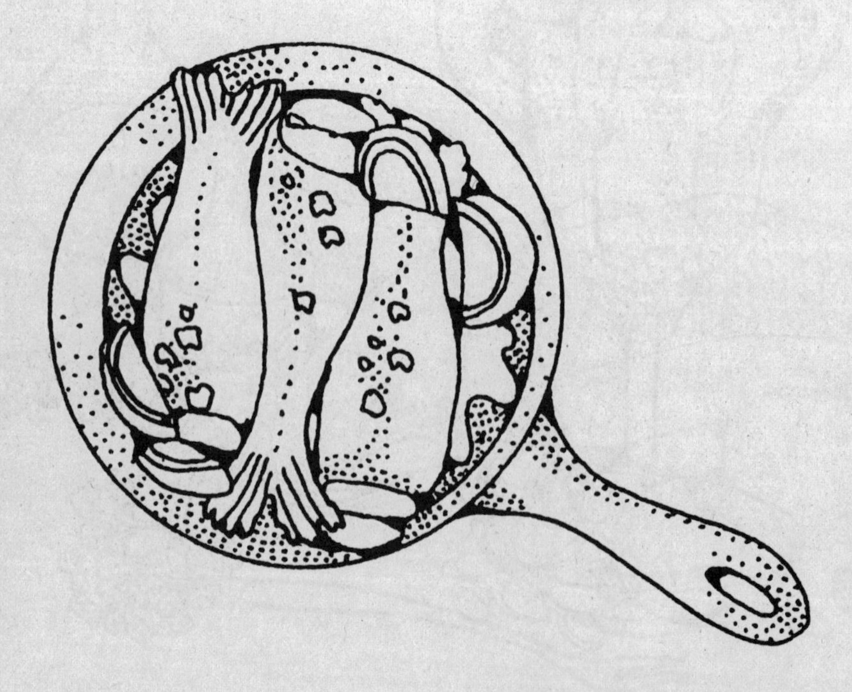

# Trout Meuniere

Makes 4 servings

4 medium trout
Lemon juice
Freshly ground black pepper
2 tablespoons butter
2 tablespoons oil
1/4 cup butter
1/4 cup lemon juice *or* white wine
1/4 cup minced fresh parsley
Sliced kiwi, avocado, *or* mango

Rub trout with lemon juice and pepper. Warm platter for fish in 200° oven. Heat butter and oil in a large frying pan over medium-high heat. Add trout and sauté until lightly browned on one side; when edges become opaque and curl slightly, 3 to 5 minutes, turn. Heat until fish flakes easily when tested with a fork in the thickest portion. Remove fish to warm platter.

Wipe out pan and melt butter. Add lemon juice and parsley all at once. Swirl and pour sauce over trout. Garnish with kiwi slices.

# Fruits

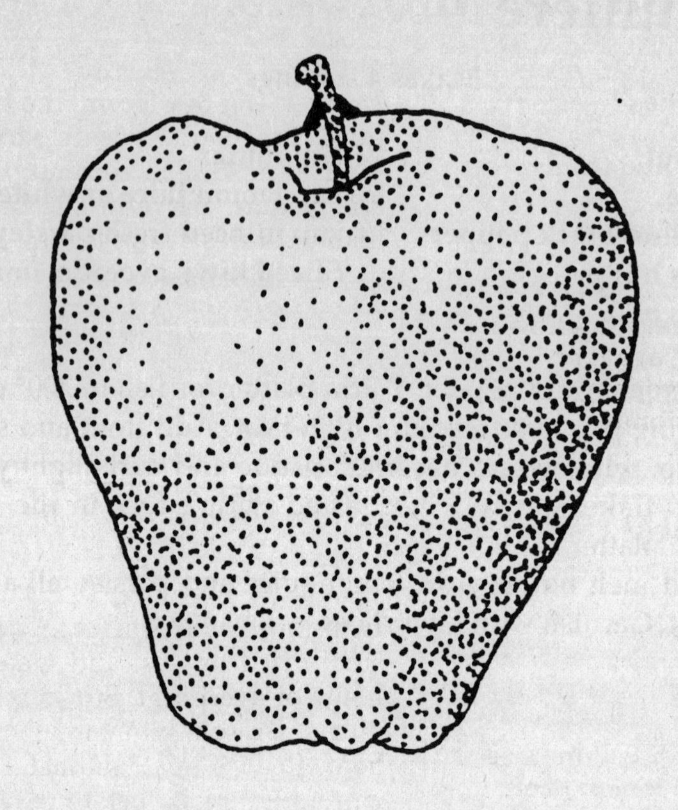

## Apple Slaw

Makes 4 servings

- 1/3 cup plain yogurt
- 1/4 cup sour cream
- 2 to 3 tablespoons minced chives
- 1 tablespoon lemon juice
- 1 teaspoon lime juice
- 1 tablespoon minced cilantro *or* parsley
- 1 teaspoon grated lemon rind
- Salt to taste
- Freshly ground pepper to taste
- 1 large red apple
- 1 cup grated peeled celery root
- 1 cup grated peeled jicama *or* turnip

In large bowl mix first 7 ingredients. Season to taste with salt and freshly ground pepper. Core apple but do not peel. Grate apple and add to yogurt mixture at once to keep apple from browning. Apple peel that does not pass through grater can be finely chopped. Blend in celery root and jicama. Let stand at room temperature for 30 minutes to blend flavors.

# Yogurt Peach Ambrosia

Makes 8 servings

**2 cups sliced peaches**
**2 bananas, sliced**
**3 oranges, peeled and thinly sliced**
**1 tablespoon fresh lemon juice**
**1 cup coconut**
**1 cup miniature marshmallows**
**1 cup unflavored yogurt *or* lemon flavored yogurt**
**Mint leaves, optional**

**In a serving bowl, combine fruit and lemon juice. Toss lightly; drain excess juice. Chill for 1 hour. Stir in coconut, marshmallows, and yogurt. Serve in sherbet glasses; garnish with fresh mint leaves, if available.**

# Fruit Soup

Makes 8 to 10 servings

**1 cup pitted prunes**
**1 cup raisins**
**1 cup dried apples**
**2 quarts water**
**2 tablespoons fresh lemon juice**
**1 teaspoon grated lemon peel**
**2 small sticks cinnamon**
**½ cup dark corn syrup**
**¼ cup instant tapioca**

**In a large saucepan, combine prunes, raisins, dried apples, and water. Set aside 8 hours or overnight. Stir in remaining ingredients. Bring mixture to a boil over medium heat. Reduce heat; simmer 1 hour. Discard cinnamon sticks before serving. Serve hot or chilled.**

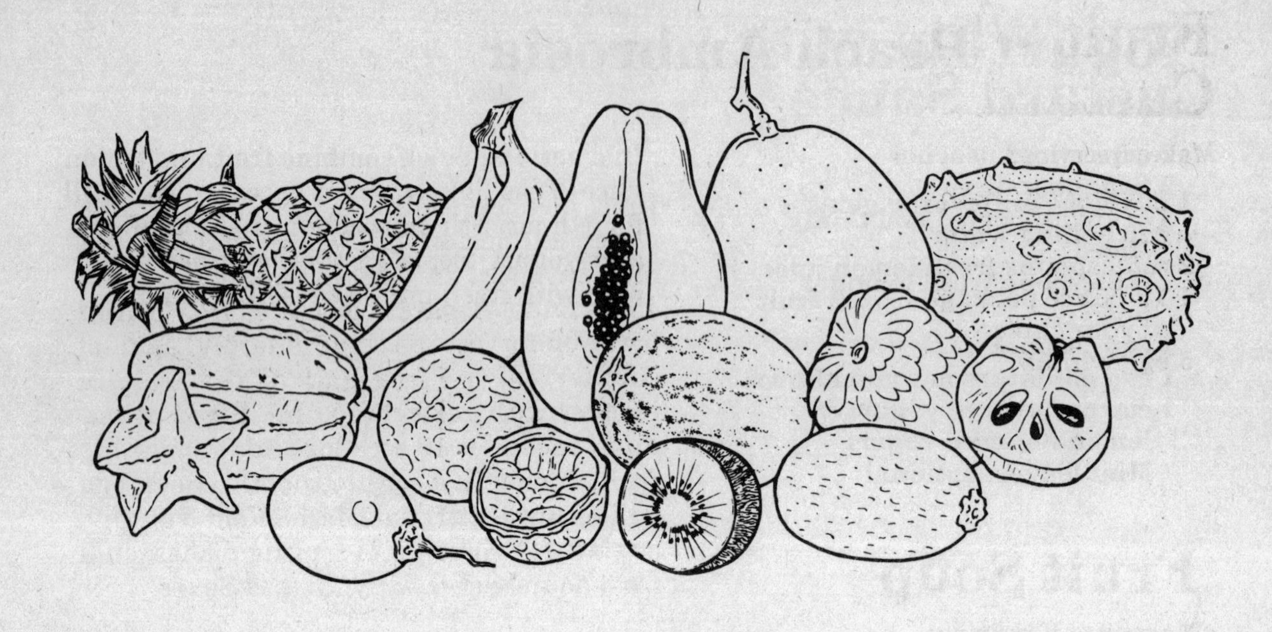

# Fresh Fruit Gelati

Makes 1 quart

2 ripe bananas
2 ripe papayas
1 tablespoon orange juice
1 tablespoon lemon juice
1 tablespoon lime juice
1 tablespoon grated orange rind
1 tablespoon grated lemon rind
1 tablespoon grated lime rind
4 cups milk
1/2 cup sugar
1 teaspoon vanilla

Combine all ingredients in food processor. Process until blended. Transfer to shallow cake pan and freeze overnight. Process again until smooth. Transfer to bowl and freeze overnight again. Serve with cookies or fresh fruit slices.

## Variations

**Rhubarb-Strawberry Gelati:** Replace bananas and papayas with 2 1/2 cups *each* sliced rhubarb and trimmed strawberries. Add additional sugar to taste.

**Pineapple-Kiwi Gelati:** Replace bananas and papayas with 1 very ripe peeled and chopped pineapple plus 4 kiwi fruits, peeled and diced.

# Fruit Whip with Custard Sauce

Makes 6 servings

1 envelope unflavored gelatin
½ cup boiling water
2 tablespoons fresh lemon juice
1 12-ounce package frozen fruit of your choice
5 egg whites

In a blender container, combine gelatin, water, and lemon juice. Cover and blend at medium speed until gelatin dissolves, about 45 seconds. Separate pieces of frozen fruit by rapping the package sharply against counter edge. Place half of the fruit in blender with gelatin mixture. Blend at medium speed for 10 seconds. Add remaining fruit; blend just until smooth. Beat egg whites until stiff peaks form. Fold fruit into egg whites. Spoon into serving dishes; chill for 3 hours. Serve with Custard Sauce.

## Custard Sauce

4 egg yolks
¼ cup sugar
⅛ teaspoon salt
1¼ cups milk
½ teaspoon rum extract

In a small, heavy saucepan, beat egg yolks lightly. Add sugar and salt; mix until well blended. Gradually stir in milk. Cook over low heat, stirring constantly, until mixture thickens and coats a metal spoon. Stir in rum extract. Cool to room temperature. Cover with plastic wrap; chill thoroughly.

# Hot Fruit Compote

Makes 4 servings

1/2 cup dry white wine, champagne, *or* sparkling cider
1 tablespoon brown sugar, optional
1/4 teaspoon ginger
1/4 teaspoon nutmeg
1/4 teaspoon cinnamon
1/2 thinly sliced lemon *or* lime
4 small peaches, apples, *or* 2 fresh pears, sliced

Combine all ingredients except fruit in a saucepan and bring to a boil. Reduce heat. Add fruit; cook and stir occasionally until tender, about 10 minutes. Serve warm.

# Pink Grapefruit Ice

Makes 4 servings

3 medium pink grapefruit, peeled, segmented, membranes removed
⅔ cup sugar
¼ cup water
3 tablespoons rum
1 cup fresh blackberries

In a food processor, process grapefruit, sugar, water, and rum until very smooth. Pour mixture into a 9 x 13-inch pan. Freeze at least 4 hours. Return mixture to processor; process until very smooth and light. Freeze again until just firm, about 45 minutes. Set aside to soften at room temperature for 10 minutes. Spoon into serving dishes; garnish with blackberries.

# Cantaloupe Fruit Boats with Honey-Lemon Dressing

Makes 4 servings

1 ripe cantaloupe *or* honeydew melon
4 peaches, pitted and sliced
1 tablespoon lemon juice
2 teaspoons lime juice
2 plums, pitted and sliced
½ cup blueberries
½ cup raspberries
1 kiwi fruit, peeled and sliced
Honey-Lemon Dressing(below)

Cut melon into 4 wedges; discard seeds. Toss peach slices with lemon and lime juice. Mix together all fruits and fill each melon wedge. Top with Honey-Lemon Dressing.

## Honey-Lemon Dressing

Makes 1 cup

1 cup plain yogurt
1 tablespoon honey
½ teaspoon dry mustard
1 teaspoon lemon juice
1 teaspoon lime juice

In a small bowl blend together all ingredients. Cover and chill until serving time.

# Fresh Fruit Compote

Makes 8 servings

½ cup water
1 cup sugar
1 cup dry white wine
½ cup white creme de menthe
1 cup fresh orange juice
¼ cup fresh lemon juice
1 pint strawberries
1 pint blueberries
4 cups peeled, sliced fresh peaches
1½ cups sour cream
½ teaspoon nutmeg
Mint sprigs

In a saucepan, combine water and sugar; bring to a boil over medium heat. Reduce heat; simmer for 5 minutes, stirring occasionally. Pour into a large glass bowl. Add wine, creme de menthe, orange juice, and lemon juice; blend well. Stir in fruits. Place in refrigerator to marinate 8 hours or overnight. Divide fruits and marinade among 8 sherbet glasses. Garnish with sour cream, nutmeg, and sprigs of mint.

# Sautéed Apples

Makes 4 servings

4 medium apples, sliced
2 tablespoons butter *or* margarine
2 tablespoons granulated sugar
Dash Cinnamon

In a skillet cook and stir apples in hot butter *or* margarine over medium-high heat for 6 to 8 minutes or until tender. Stir in sugar and cinnamon. Serve hot.

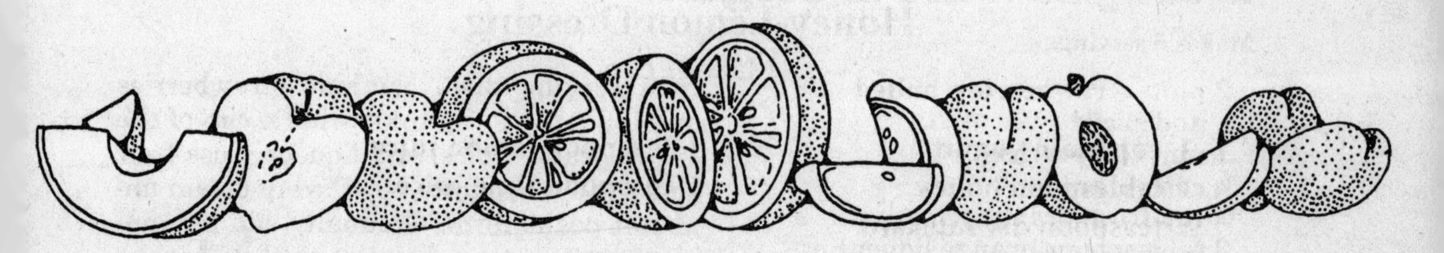

# Chilled Fruit Soup

Makes 4 servings

- 5 large ripe bananas, peeled and quartered *or* 1 bag frozen peaches *or* nectarines, thawed
- 2 tablespoons sugar
- ½ cup Neufchatel cheese
- ¼ cup plain yogurt
- 2 tablespoons orange juice concentrate, thawed
- 1 tablespoon lemon juice
- 2 to 3 tablespoons sweet *or* cream sherry
- Kiwi fruit slices
- Fresh mint sprigs

In a blender or food processor blend all ingredients, except kiwi and mint, until smooth. Taste and add additional lemon or sherry as desired. Pour into a serving bowl; cover and chill. Garnish with kiwi fruit slices and fresh mint sprigs.

# Berry Swirl Delight

Makes 6 servings

- 2 pints strawberries, hulled and sliced
- 1 pint blueberries
- ¾ cup sugar
- ¼ cup fresh orange juice
- 3 tablespoons orange liqueur *or* Triple Sec to taste
- 1 cup heavy cream

In a serving dish, combine strawberries and blueberries. Sprinkle with ½ cup of the sugar, orange juice, and liqueur. Toss fruit gently. In a separate bowl, whip cream until soft peaks form. Gradually add remaining sugar; continue beating until stiff peaks form and sugar dissolves. Swirl cream into berries for a marbled effect.

# Cherry Soup

Makes 8 servings

**3 16-ounce cans pitted tart cherries, drained, juice reserved**
**1 cup water**
**¼ cup sugar**
**½ teaspoon cinnamon**
**½ teaspoon allspice**
**¼ teaspoon nutmeg**
**1 cup dry red wine**
**1 pint heavy cream** *or* **half-and-half**

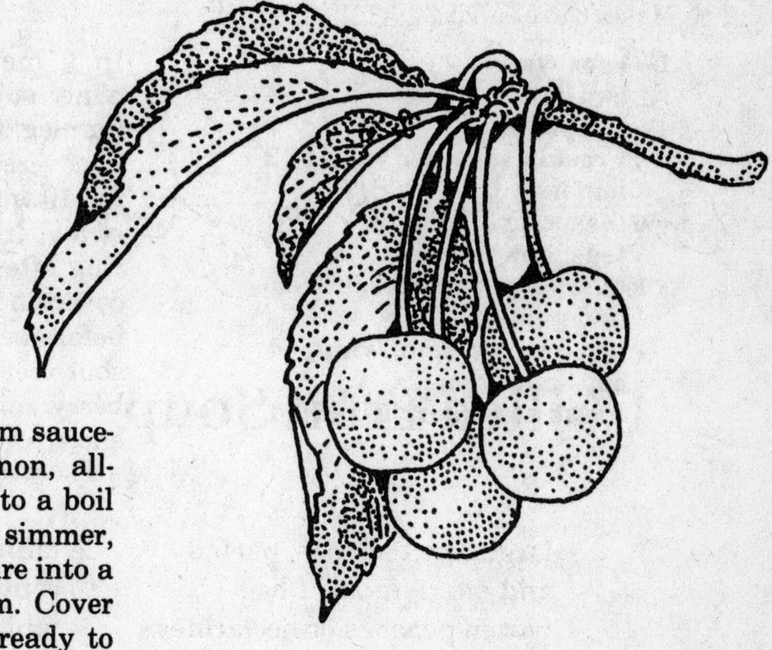

Chop cherries and place in a medium saucepan. Stir in water, sugar, cinnamon, allspice, and nutmeg. Bring mixture to a boil over medium heat. Reduce heat; simmer, covered, for 4 minutes. Ladle mixture into a tureen. Stir in red wine and cream. Cover with plastic wrap and chill until ready to serve.

# Layered Fruits with Citrus-Honey Ricotta

Makes 4 servings

**1 cup ricotta cheese**
**1 cup cream cheese**
**Grated rind of 1 lemon**
**Grated rind of 1 orange**
**Grated rind of 1 lime**
**1 to 2 tablespoons lemon juice**
**1 to 2 tablespoons orange juice**
**1 to 2 tablespoons lime juice**
**¼ cup honey**
**2 to 3 tablespoons fresh chopped mint, optional**
**Sliced fresh fruits (berries, bananas, plums, peaches)**
**Fresh mint leaves, optional**

Combine cheeses, fruit zest, honey, and chopped mint, if desired; blend well. Layer mixture with sliced fruit in parfait glasses. Chill before serving. Garnish with fresh mint sprigs.

# Strawberry Soup

Makes 6 to 8 servings

**1½ cups water**
**1 cup dry red wine**
**½ cup sugar**
**Freshly squeezed juice of 2 lemons**
**½ teaspoon cinnamon**
**¼ teaspoon nutmeg**
**1 quart strawberries, hulled and pureed**
**1 cup heavy cream, whipped**
**¼ cup sour cream**
**Fresh strawberries, sliced**

In a medium saucepan, combine water, wine, sugar, lemon juice, cinnamon, and nutmeg. Over medium heat, bring mixture, uncovered, to a boil. Reduce heat; simmer for 10 minutes, stirring occasionally. Add strawberry puree; simmer 10 minutes, stirring often. Cool at room temperature, then cover and refrigerate until well chilled. Just before serving, combine heavy cream and sour cream in a small bowl. Add to strawberry mixture; blend well. Garnish with sliced strawberries.

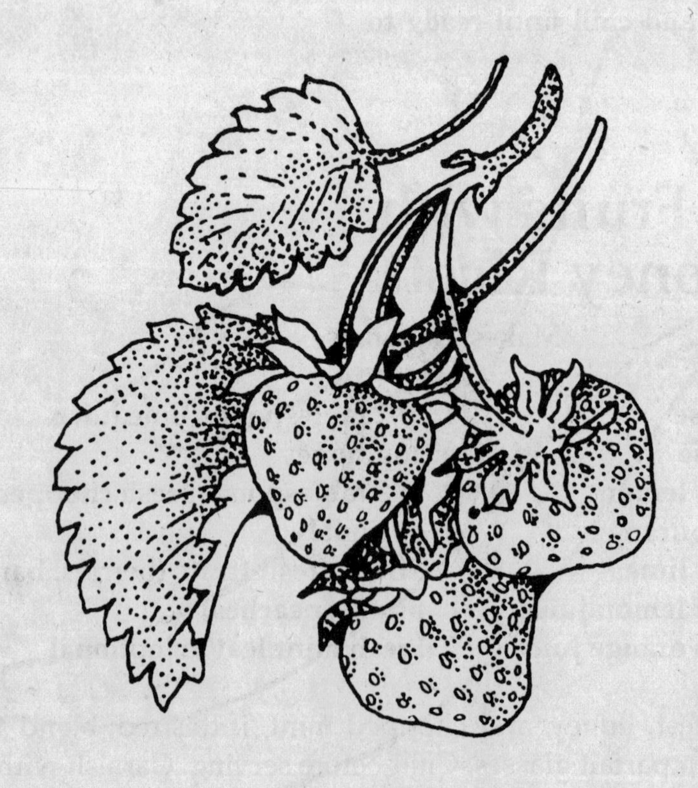

# Bananas with Rum Cream

Makes 4 servings

- **1 egg, separated**
- **1/4 cup brown sugar**
- **1/2 of a 4-ounce container frozen whipped dessert topping, thawed**
- **1 tablespoon dark rum**
- **4 small bananas, sliced**
- **Chocolate curls, optional**

In a small mixer bowl beat egg white until soft peaks form; gradually add half of the brown sugar, beating until stiff peaks form. Transfer to a clean bowl. In the same mixer bowl, beat egg yolk until thick and lemon-colored; beat in remaining brown sugar and rum. Fold egg white and dessert topping into yolk mixture. Chill until serving time. To serve, place sliced bananas in 4 dessert dishes. Spoon rum cream over fruit. Garnish with choclate curls, if desired.

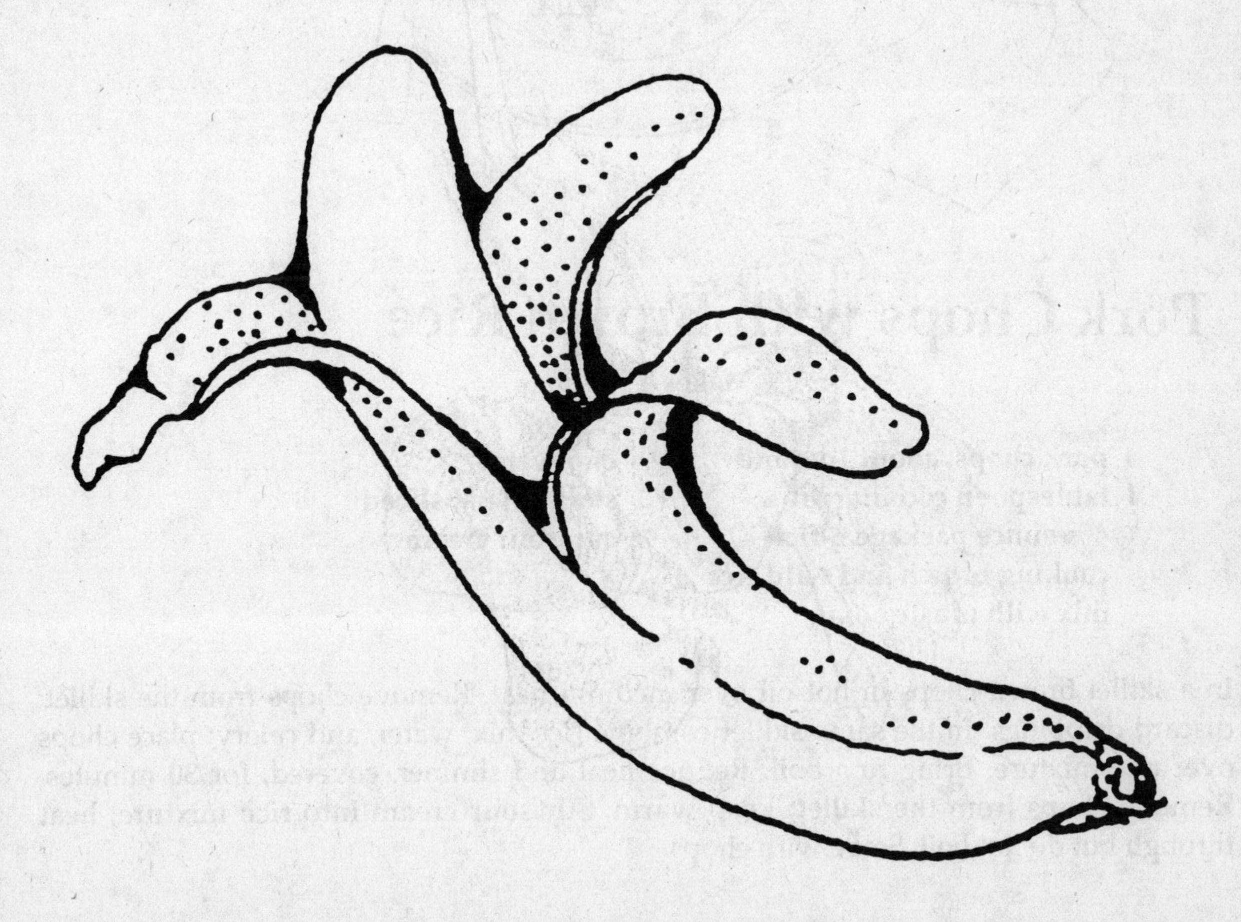

## Pork Chops with Brown Rice

Makes 4 servings

**4 pork chops, about 1 pound**
**1 tablespoon cooking oil**
**1 4 5/8-ounce package quick-cooking brown and wild rice mix with mushrooms**
**1 1/3 cup water**
**1 stalk celery, sliced**
**1/2 cup sour cream**

In a skillet brown chops in hot oil over medium heat. Remove chops from the skillet; discard drippings. In the same skillet combine rice mix, water, and celery; place chops over rice mixture. Bring to a boil. Reduce heat and simmer, covered, for 30 minutes. Remove chops from the skillet; keep warm. Stir sour cream into rice mixture; heat through but do not boil. Serve with chops.

# Toad-in-the-Hole

Makes 8 servings

**4 eggs, beaten**
**½ teaspoon salt**
**1 cup milk**
**2 cups all-purpose flour, sifted**
**2 pounds pork sausages, cut in ¾-inch pieces**

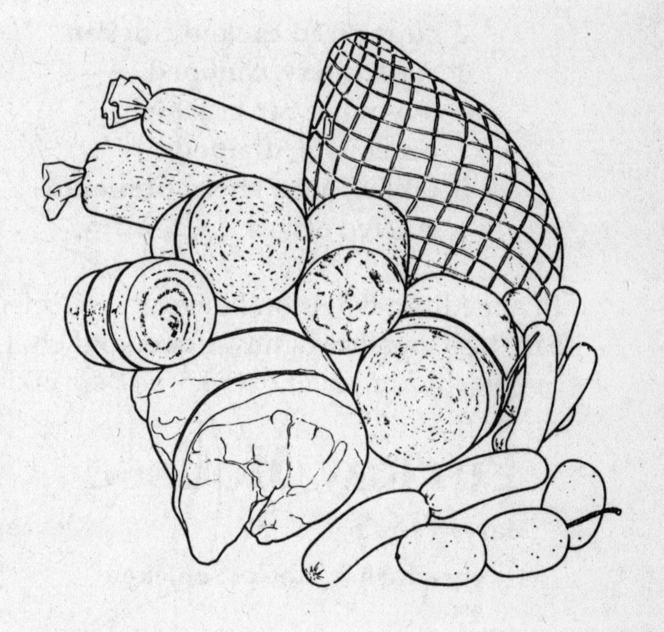

Preheat oven to 425° F. In a large mixing bowl, combine eggs, salt, and milk. Blend in flour. Set aside for 15 minutes. In a heavy skillet over medium-high heat, sauté sausage. Distribute drippings among eight 3-inch pie tins. Pour a thin layer (about ¼ inch) of batter into each tin. Bake for 5 minutes or until set. Add sausage; top with remaining batter. Bake for about 25 minutes or until puffed up and browned. Serve at once.

# Poached Chicken and Vermicelli in Wine

Makes 4 servings

**1 teaspoon butter *or* margarine**
**1 teaspoon oil**
**½ pound mushrooms, sliced**
**4 boned chicken breasts, skinned and halved**
**¼ teaspoon salt**
**½ teaspoon tarragon**
**⅛ teaspoon pepper**
**2 tablespoons minced fresh parsley**
**¾ cup dry white wine**
**1 teaspoon arrowroot, optional**
**8 ounces vermicelli, cooked and drained**

Melt butter *or* margarine and oil in a large skillet over medium-high heat. Sauté mushrooms and chicken until golden brown. Sprinkle with salt, tarragon, pepper, and parsley. Pour wine over chicken. Cover and simmer for 25 to 30 minutes. Remove chicken to serving platter. Deglaze skillet with a little water; thicken with one teaspoon arrowroot, if desired. Serve sauce with chicken and prepared vermicelli.

# Chicken Salad Croissants

Makes 4 servings

- 2 cups diced cooked chicken
- 1 stalk celery, chopped
- 1 8½-ounce can crushed pineapple, drained
- 2 tablespoons sliced pimiento-stuffed olives
- ½ cup mayonnaise
- Dash salt
- Leaf lettuce
- 4 croissants, split
- ¼ cup chopped cashews

In a medium bowl combine chicken, celery, pineapple, and olives. Add mayonnaise and salt; toss together lightly. Cover and chill. To serve, place a lettuce leaf in each croissant. Spoon chicken salad over lettuce; sprinkle with cashews.

# Turkey Mousse

Makes 4 servings

- **1½ cups turkey stock *or* chicken stock**
- **1 package unflavored gelatin**
- **1½ cups minced, cooked turkey**
- **¼ cup mayonnaise**
- **1 small onion, minced**
- **1 stalk celery, minced**
- **1 teaspoon celery salt**
- **½ teaspoon curry powder**
- **¾ cup heavy cream, whipped**
- **Fresh vegetables**

Lightly oil a 1-quart mold. Place ½ cup of the turkey stock in a small heatproof bowl or cup. Sprinkle gelatin over stock; let soften for about 1 minute. Set bowl in a pan of simmering water; stir constantly until gelatin dissolves. Remove from heat. In a mixing bowl, combine remaining ingredients, except heavy cream and fresh vegetables. Blend in dissolved gelatin. Refrigerate until mixture begins to set. Fold in whipped cream. Spoon mixture into mold. Cover lightly; chill overnight. When ready to serve, unmold and garnish with fresh vegetables.

# Gingered Chicken with Apples

Makes 4 servings

- 1 tablespoon safflower oil *or* vegetable oil
- 2½ pounds chicken, cut into pieces
- ¼ cup Cognac
- ½ cup evaporated skim milk
- ½ cup non-fat milk
- 1 tablespoon chopped gingerroot *or* ½ teaspoon ground ginger
- ½ teaspoon nutmeg
- 1½ cups thinly sliced tart apples
- 1 teaspoon arrowroot, optional
- Toasted slivered almonds
- Chopped candied ginger

Heat oil in a large skillet. Add chicken, skin side down; brown well on all sides. Remove and set aside. Deglaze pan with Cognac. Flambé if desired. Return browned chicken to skillet.

To make cream sauce, combine next 5 ingredients. Add to skillet and gently simmer 20 to 30 minutes. Remove chicken to serving platter. Add apples to skillet. Cook until just tender, 1 to 2 minutes. Thicken with arrowroot, if desired. Serve apples and sauce over chicken. Garnish with almonds and candied ginger.

# Oven-Fried Chicken Nuggets

Makes 8 to 10 servings

- 1 cup seasoned bread crumbs
- ½ teaspoon garlic powder
- 3 chicken breasts, skinned, boned, and cut into 1-inch pieces
- ½ cup butter, melted

Preheat oven to 400° F. In a shallow bowl, mix bread crumbs with garlic powder. Dip chicken pieces into melted butter; roll in bread crumbs, and place on a baking sheet. Bake for 10 to 12 minutes. Serve hot with Tartar Sauce.

## Tartar Sauce

- 1 cup mayonnaise
- 2 green onions, chopped
- 2 teaspoons capers
- 1 medium dill pickle, minced
- 1 clove garlic, minced

In a small bowl, combine all ingredients. Stir until well mixed. Place in a covered container; chill until ready to serve.

# Greek Stir-Fry

Makes 4 servings

1 tablespoon olive oil *or* vegetable oil
1 pound lamb, cubed (leg, shoulder, or shank)
1 red onion, diced
2 to 3 cloves garlic, minced
1 cup red wine
1 cup beef broth
1/4 cup minced fresh parsley
1 to 2 teaspoons chopped fresh mint *or* parsley
1 teaspoon oregano
1 small eggplant, diced
1 teaspoon arrowroot, optional
Sliced black olives
Parsley *or* mint

Heat oil in a wok or skillet. Add lamb, onion, and garlic; sauté until lamb is browned. Deglaze wok with wine. Add broth, parsley, mint, and oregano; simmer about 25 minutes. Add eggplant during the last 10 minutes of cooking time. Reduce liquid over high heat or thicken by stirring in arrowroot, if desired. Garnish with olives and sprinkle with parsley.

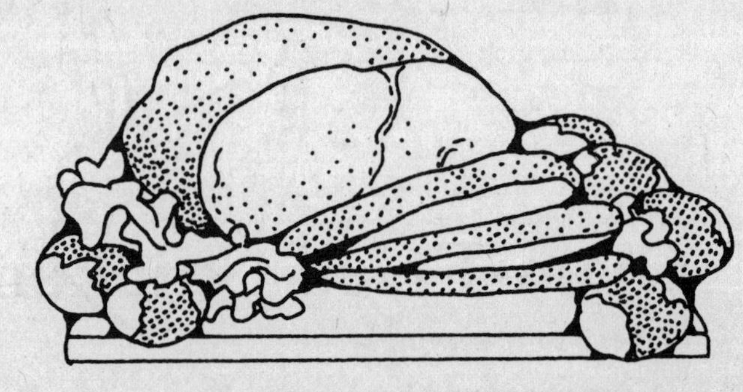

# Beef Burgundy

Makes 8 servings

2 slices bacon, chopped
2 pounds beef tenderloin, cut into thin strips
1 tablespoon flour
1/4 teaspoon thyme
1/2 cup burgundy
1/2 cup beef broth
1/4 cup tomato paste
1 bay leaf
2 tablespoons butter
1/2 pound mushrooms, sliced
16 small frozen onions

In a large, heavy skillet over medium heat, sauté bacon until crisp. Add tenderloin; sprinkle with flour and thyme. Add burgundy, broth, tomato paste, and bay leaf; stir until well mixed. Reduce heat to low, cover, and simmer until almost tender, about 1½ hours.

In another skillet, melt butter; add mushrooms and onions; sauté until golden. Add to beef mixture; stir until well mixed.

# Veal and Artichoke Sauté

Makes 4 servings

- **1 pound veal *or* turkey cutlets, cut to finger lengths**
- **Flour**
- **Salt and pepper**
- **1/2 teaspoon sage**
- **2 tablespoons butter *or* margarine**
- **1 9-ounce package frozen artichoke hearts, thawed**
- **1/2 cup dry white wine *or* vermouth**
- **1/2 cup chicken broth**
- **1/4 cup half-and-half *or* whipping cream**
- **Grated Parmesan cheese**

Dust veal lightly with flour and seasonings. Sauté in butter over medium-high heat 4 to 6 minutes. Transfer to serving platter and keep warm. Add artichokes, wine, broth, and half-and-half to skillet. Cover and simmer until artichokes are tender. Pour over veal and dust with cheese.

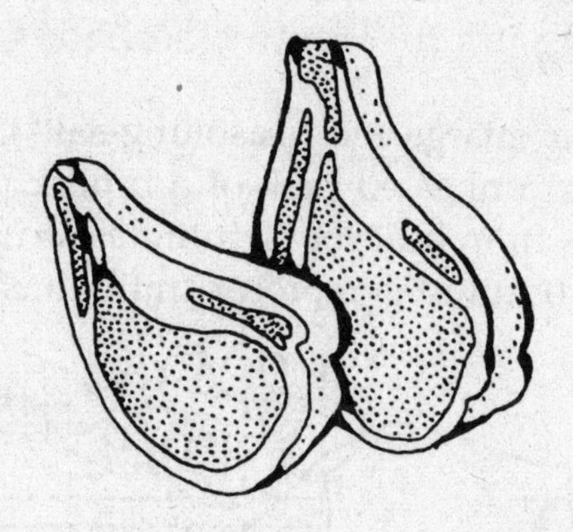

# Mustard-Broiled Pork Chops

Makes 4 servings

- **1/4 cup Dijon-style mustard**
- **4 pork loin chops, 3/4 inch thick, trimmed**
- **Freshly ground pepper to taste**

Preheat broiler. Spread half of the mustard evenly over chops. Broil 6 inches away from heat source for 8 to 10 minutes. Turn chops; spread with remaining mustard. Grind pepper over chops. Broil another 10 minutes.

# Saucy Canadian Bacon

16 slices Canadian bacon
½ cup firmly packed light brown sugar
1 teaspoon dry mustard
1 tablespoon cider vinegar

Sauté Canadian bacon. Place on a serving platter. In a small saucepan, heat sugar, mustard, and vinegar over medium heat until sugar melts and sauce is hot. Drizzle sauce over bacon.

# Butter-Broiled Chicken

Makes 4 servings

6 tablespoons butter *or* margarine, melted
1/4 teaspoon seasoning salt
1/4 teaspoon dried oregano, crushed
Dash Garlic powder
Dash paprika
8 to 10 skinless chicken breasts

Preheat broiler. Combine butter *or* margarine, seasoning salt, oregano, garlic powder, and paprika. Place chicken on an unheated rack of a broiler pan. Brush lightly with butter mixture. Broil 5 to 6 inches from heat for 10 minutes, brushing occasionally with butter mixture. Turn; broil for 10 minutes more or until chicken is tender, brushing occasionally.

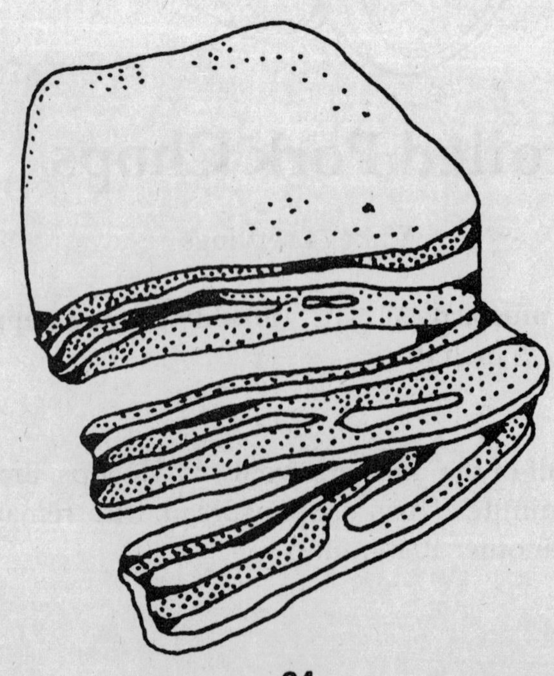

# Chicken Jambalaya

Makes 4 servings

**2 to 3 cloves garlic, minced**
**1/2 cup chopped red onion**
**1 stalk celery, sliced**
**2 hot chorizos, casings removed and broken up**
**2 tablespoons olive oil *or* vegetable oil**
**1 cup chicken broth**
**1 cup white wine**
**1 cup long-grain white rice**
**1 16-ounce can stewed tomatoes, chopped**
**1 teaspoon thyme *or* oregano leaves**
**1/2 teaspoon turmeric**
**1/4 teaspoon red pepper**
**1/2 20-ounce package frozen peas**
**1 pound medium-size raw shrimp, in shells *or* frozen shrimp**

Sauté first 4 ingredients 3 to 5 minutes in hot oil. Add next 7 ingredients. Bring to a boil. Reduce heat; cover and simmer 15 minutes. Add peas and shrimp. Cover and cook 5 minutes. Toss with a fork to fluff rice and distribute shrimp.
*Note:* 8 fresh mussels or clams may be substituted for 1/2 pound of shrimp.

# Lamb Chops Persillade

Makes 4 servings

**4 lamb loin chops,1 inch thick**
**2 cloves garlic, minced and stirred to paste**
**1 tablespoon butter**
**3 tablespoons minced shallots**
**1/3 cup fine bread crumbs**
**1/3 cup minced fresh parsley**
**1 teaspoon tarragon, basil, *or* thyme**
**Freshly ground pepper**
**Grated Parmesan cheese**

Line broiler pan with foil to collect drippings. Rub chops with garlic paste. Broil 4 inches from heat source for 6 to 8 minutes on each side. Melt butter in a saucepan; sauté shallots and bread crumbs until golden brown. Remove from heat. Stir in parsley, herbs, and drippings from lamb chops. Add pepper and cheese to taste. Spread over one side of chops before serving.

# Raspberry Glazed Chicken

Makes 4 servings

- 1 2-pound whole roasting chicken
- Cooking oil
- 1/3 cup raspberry jelly
- 2 tablespoons lemon juice
- 1 tablespoon butter *or* margarine
- 1/4 teaspoon salt
- Dash ground cinnamon
- 1 tablespoon cold water
- 2 teaspoons cornstarch

Thoroughly rinse chicken; pat dry with paper towel. Place chicken, breast side up, on a rack in a shallow roasting pan. Rub skin with oil. Insert a meat thermometer in the center of the inside thigh muscle but not touching bone. Roast, uncovered, in a 375° oven for 1 1/4 to 1 1/2 hours or until thermometer registers 185°. In a small saucepan over low heat stir together jelly, lemon juice, butter *or* margarine, salt, and cinnamon until jelly melts. Combine water and cornstarch; stir into jelly mixture. Cook and stir over medium heat until thick and bubbly. Cook and stir 1 to 2 minutes more. Brush on chicken several times during the last 15 minutes of roasting.

# Chicken Puffs

Makes 1 dozen pastries

- 1/2 package (10 ounces) puff pastry sheets
- 1 tablespoon butter
- 1 small red onion, minced
- 2 teaspoons curry
- 1 teaspoon chopped chutney
- 1 tablespoon chopped walnuts *or* almonds
- 1 tablespoon shredded coconut
- 1/2 cup half-and-half
- 1 cup chopped cooked chicken

Roll out one sheet puff pastry. Cut out 1 1/2-inch rounds with fluted cookie cutter. Bake in oven according to package directions. Melt butter in a large saucepan. Sauté onion until golden. Stir in curry, chutney, nuts, and coconut; cook 3 to 5 minutes. Add half-and-half and bring to a boil. Simmer 5 minutes. Add chicken and blend well. Serve warm or cold on puff pastry shells.

# Chicken in Red Pepper Butter

Makes 4 servings

**4 boneless skinless chicken breasts, halved**
**2 tablespoons butter *or* margarine**
**2 tablespoons vegetable oil**
**2 cloves garlic, minced**
**Red Pepper Butter (below)**

Pound breasts to a thickness of 1/4 inch. Heat butter *or* margarine, oil, and garlic in sauté pan. Sauté chicken breasts over medium-high heat, 3 to 5 minutes per side. Transfer to platter and keep warm in oven. Serve breasts with Red Pepper Butter.

## Red Pepper Butter

Makes approximately 3 cups

**2 tablespoons butter**
**2 medium shallots, minced**
**2 1/2 medium red bell peppers, sliced**
**3 tablespoons raspberry vinegar *or* red wine vinegar**
**1/4 cup fresh lemon juice**
**1/2 cup dry white wine *or* vermouth**
**1 cup unsalted butter, melted**

Melt 2 tablespoons butter in medium saucepan; sauté shallots and peppers. Stew over low heat, stirring often, until shallots and peppers are softened, about 8 minutes. Add vinegar and cook on high heat until reduced by two-thirds. Add lemon juice and wine. Reduce by half. Transfer to food processor and purée until smooth, 1 to 1 1/2 minutes. Add 1 cup melted butter in a thin stream while machine is running. Process 20 seconds longer. Just before serving, whisk sauce over low heat until hot to the touch. Do not simmer. *Note:* Red Pepper Butter can be prepared 3 hours ahead of time. Cover and store at room temperature until serving time.

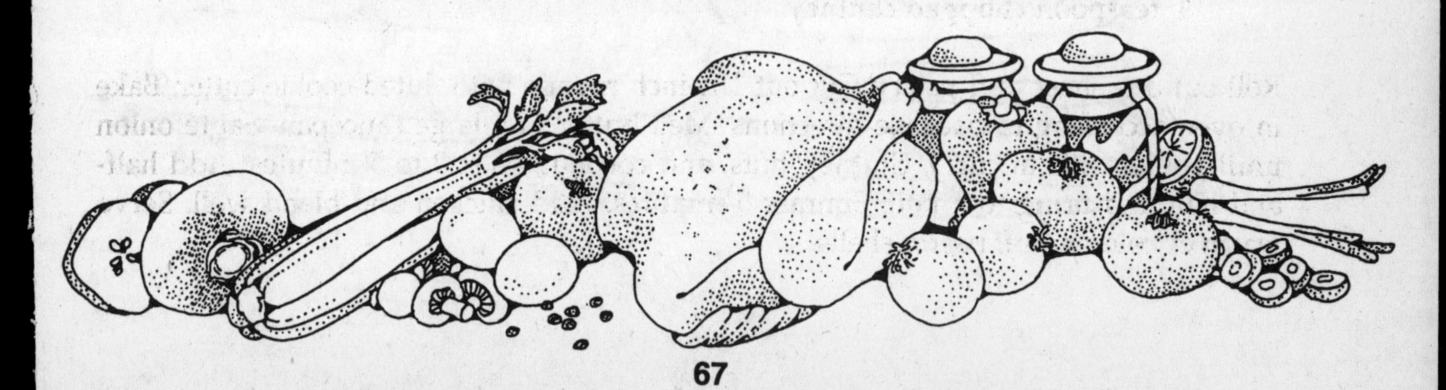

## Chocolate Chip Buttermilk Pancakes

Makes 4 servings

**1 cup sifted all-purpose flour**
**¾ teaspoon baking soda**
**¼ teaspoon salt**
**1 egg, lightly beaten**
**1 cup buttermilk**
**2 tablespoons melted butter**
**1 cup semisweet chocolate chips**

In a mixing bowl, stir together flour, soda, and salt. In a separate bowl, beat egg with buttermilk and melted butter until well blended. Add buttermilk mixture all at once to dry ingredients; stir just until dry ingredients are moistened. Stir in chocolate chips. Cover batter and set aside at room temperature for 20 minutes. Lightly butter a pancake griddle. Drop batter, about 1 tablespoon for each pancake, onto hot griddle. Bake pancakes until bubbles form on top and edges are dry. Turn and bake until pancakes are cooked through.

# Oven Pancake

Makes 4 servings

- 6 eggs
- 1 cup milk
- 1/4 cup butter *or* margarine, melted
- 1 cup all-purpose flour
- 3/4 teaspoon salt
- Melted butter *or* margarine
- Sifted powdered sugar

In a blender combine eggs, milk, and melted butter *or* margarine. Cover and blend on low speed until mixed. Add flour and salt; cover and blend on medium speed until smooth. Pour into a well-greased 13 x 9 x 2-inch baking dish.

Bake at 450° for 20 to 22 minutes or until puffed and golden brown. Drizzle with melted butter and sprinkle with powdered sugar. Serve immediately.

# Potato Pancakes with Sour Cream

Makes 6 to 8 servings

- **4 medium potatoes, peeled and grated**
- **1 onion, grated**
- **1 egg, lightly beaten**
- **½ teaspoon salt**
- **½ teaspoon baking soda**
- **4 to 6 tablespoons butter**
- **2 cups sour cream**

Press potatoes with a paper towel to remove as much liquid as possible. In a large mixing bowl, stir together potato, onion, and egg until well mixed. Blend in salt and soda. In a large, heavy skillet, heat 1 tablespoon of the butter until it sizzles. Drop batter by heaping tablespoonfuls into skillet. Cook until golden brown on one side. Turn; continue cooking until pancakes are cooked through, adding butter as needed. Serve hot with sour cream.

# Seafood Crêpes with Mornay Sauce

Makes 16 crepes

**4 tablespoons butter *or* margarine**
**1 medium onion, chopped**
**½ pound mushrooms, sliced**
**2 cups cooked seafood: scallops, shrimp *or* crab**
**Mornay Sauce**
**½ cup grated Parmesan cheese**
**2 tablespoons minced fresh parsley**
**½ teaspoon salt**
**¼ teaspoon white pepper**
**16 Luncheon Crepes (this page)**

Preheat oven to 375° F. Butter a large, shallow baking dish. In a large skillet over medium heat, melt butter. Add onion and mushrooms; sauté until vegetables are tender. Stir in seafood. Blend in ¾ cup of the Mornay Sauce, ¼ cup of the Parmesan cheese, parsley, salt, and pepper. Spoon about 2 tablespoons of the filling down the center of unbrowned side of each crepe. Roll up and place seam side down in casserole. Repeat with remaining crepes. Top with remaining sauce and Parmesan cheese. Bake for 15 minutes.

## Mornay Sauce

**3 tablespoons butter *or* margarine**
**3 tablespoons all-purpose flour**
**2 cups milk**
**2 tablespoons dry white wine**
**2 tablespoons grated Swiss cheese**
**Salt and pepper to taste**
**1 egg yolk mixed with ½ cup half-and-half**

In a small saucepan over medium heat, melt butter. Blend in flour. Stir in milk. Cook, stirring constantly, until sauce thickens. Add wine and cheese; blend well. Season with salt and pepper. Remove from heat. Add egg yolk mixture, blend well.

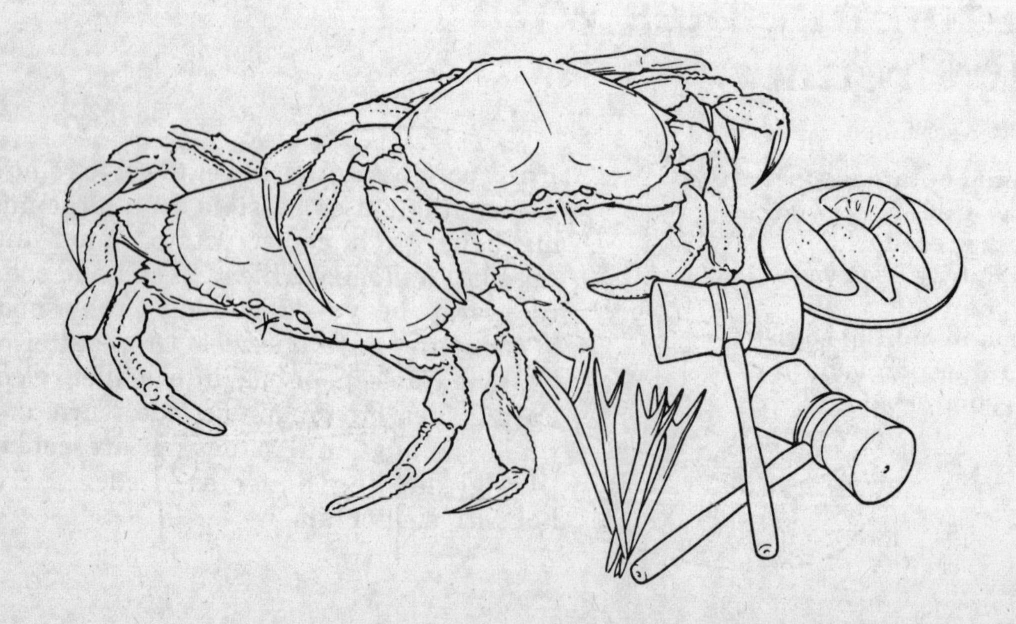

# Manicotti Crêpes

Makes about 18 crepes

**¼ cup olive oil *or* salad oil**
**1 large onion, thinly sliced**
**2 cloves garlic, minced**
**1 2-pound can Italian tomatoes**
**1 6-ounce can tomato paste**
**1½ cups water**
**1 teaspoon honey**
**2 tablespoons minced fresh parsley**
**1 teaspoon basil**
**1 teaspoon oregano**
**Salt and pepper to taste**

In a large saucepan over medium heat, heat oil. Add onion and garlic; sauté until onion is tender. Stir in tomatoes, tomato paste, water, honey, parsley, basil, oregano, salt, and pepper. Bring mixture to a boil. Reduce heat to simmer and continue cooking, stirring occasionally, for 45 minutes.

**2 pounds ricotta cheese**
**½ pound mozzarella cheese, shredded**
**¼ cup grated Parmesan cheese**
**2 eggs**
**1 tablespoon minced fresh parsley**
**Salt and pepper to taste**
**16 Luncheon Crepes (page 24)**
**2 tablespoons grated Parmesan cheese**

Preheat oven to 350° F. In a large mixing bowl, stir together cheeses, eggs, parsley, salt, and pepper until well mixed. Spoon a thin layer of sauce over the bottom of a 9 x 13-inch casserole. Spoon about 2 tablespoons of the cheese mixture along the center of each crepe; roll up. Arrange in casserole seam side down. Cover generously with sauce. (Reserve unused sauce for use in other Italian dishes.) Sprinkle with 2 tablespoons Parmesan cheese. Bake, uncovered, for 15 minutes or until heated through.

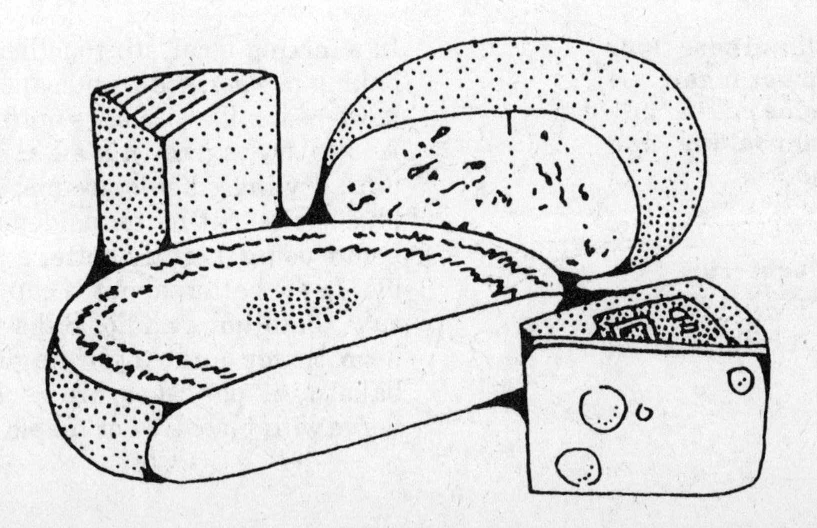

# Scandinavian Pancakes

Makes 6 servings

**1 cup all-purpose flour**
**1 teaspoon sugar**
**2 teaspoons grated orange peel**
**4 egg yolks**
**2 cups milk**
**4 tablespoons sour cream**
**4 egg whites**
**Lingonberry sauce** *or*
**raspberry sauce**

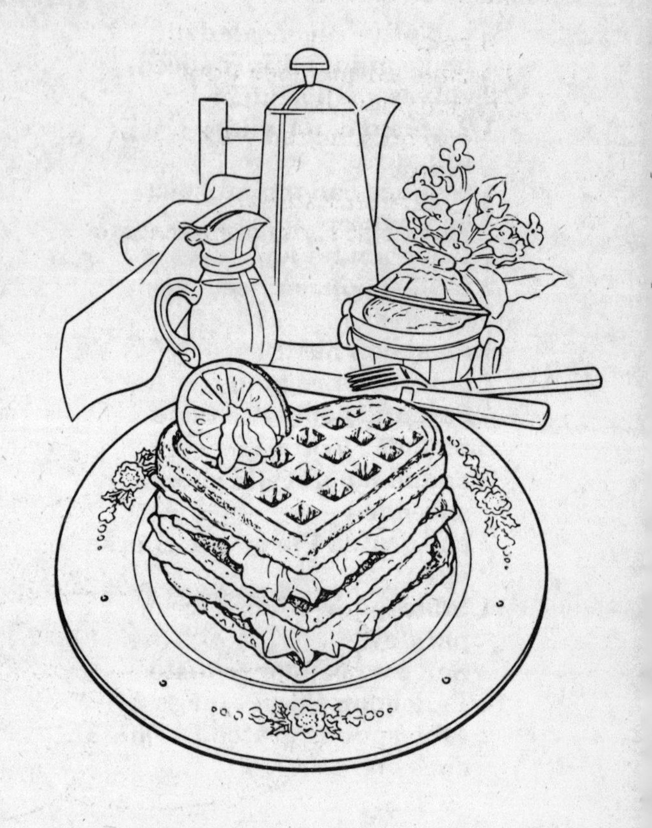

In a mixing bowl, stir together flour, sugar, and orange peel. In a separate bowl, beat together egg yolks, milk, and sour cream. Add milk mixture to dry ingredients; blend until batter is smooth. In a small, deep bowl, beat egg whites until stiff peaks form. Fold egg whites into batter. Generously butter a large, heavy skillet. Drop batter by tablespoonfuls into hot skillet; bake until lightly browned. Turn pancake and lightly brown the other side. Serve with lingonberry sauce.

# Blueberry Pancakes

Makes 6 servings

**2 cups all-purpose flour**
**1 tablespoon sugar**
**3 teaspoons baking powder**
**½ teaspoon baking soda**
**¼ teaspoon salt**
**2½ cups milk**
**2 eggs**
**2 cups blueberries**
**Blueberry syrup** *or*
**maple syrup**

In a mixing bowl, stir together flour, sugar, baking powder, soda, and salt. In a separate bowl, beat milk with eggs until well blended. Add to dry ingredients all at once; stir just until dry ingredients are moistened. Stir in blueberries. Set batter aside for 30 minutes before using. Lightly butter a pancake griddle. Ladle batter, about ¼ cup for each pancake, onto hot griddle. Bake until bubbles form on top and edges are dry. Turn and bake until pancakes are cooked through. Serve with blueberry or maple syrup.

# Basic Blintzes

• Makes 18 blintzes

**4 eggs**
**1¼ cups all-purpose flour**
**¼ teaspoon salt**
**1 cup milk mixed with ½ cup water**
**1 teaspoon vanilla**
**Butter at room temperature**

In a large bowl, beat eggs until lemon-colored. Stir together flour and salt; add to eggs alternately with milk; blend well. Set aside at room temperature for 20 minutes. In an 8-inch skillet, heat ½ teaspoon butter. Add about 2 tablespoons of the batter. Immediately tilt pan from side to side so that batter covers the bottom of the pan. Cook until lightly browned on one side. Turn out onto a paper towel. Repeat with remaining batter.

# Pineapple Blintzes

Makes about 18 blintzes

**16 ounces cream cheese**
**16 ounces dry cottage cheese**
**¾ cup sugar**
**1 egg**
**2 teaspoons grated orange peel**
**1 teaspoon vanilla**
**½ cup drained crushed pineapple**
**5 tablespoons butter *or* margarine**
**18 Basic Blintzes (this page)**
**Sour cream**

In a mixing bowl, combine cream cheese and cottage cheese; blend well. Stir in remaining ingredients, except butter, blintzes and sour cream. Spoon about 2 tablespoons of the filling along one "side" of each blintze. Fold over edges to form a rectangle. Roll up. In a large, heavy skillet, heat butter until it sizzles. Fry blintzes, turning once, until lightly browned on both sides. Serve hot with sour cream.

# Luncheon Crêpes

Makes 16 crepes

**1 cup milk**
**½ cup water**
**2 eggs**
**2 tablespoons butter, melted**
**2 tablespoons vegetable oil**
**1 cup all-purpose flour**
**¼ teaspoon salt**

In a mixing bowl, combine all ingredients; blend until smooth. Cover batter; set aside at room temperature for 30 minutes. Butter or oil a crepe pan. Heat pan until butter sizzles or oil is hot. Add 2 tablespoons of the batter. Immediately tilt pan from side to side so that batter covers the bottom of the pan. Cook about 1½ minutes or until crepe is lightly browned on one side. Turn out onto a paper towel. Repeat with remaining batter.

# Chicken Crêpes with Sour Cream

Makes 16 crepes

**4 tablespoons butter** *or* **margarine**
**1 onion, chopped**
**½ cup chopped celery**
**3 cups diced cooked chicken**
**1 cup sour cream**
**½ teaspoon tarragon**
**Salt and pepper to taste**
**16 Luncheon Crepes (page 24)**
**Sour cream**
**Parsley sprigs**

Preheat oven to 375° F. Grease a large, shallow baking dish. In a large, heavy skillet, heat butter. Add onion and celery; sauté over medium heat until vegetables are tender. Stir in chicken, sour cream, tarragon, salt, and pepper. Spoon about 2 tablespoons of the filling down the center of unbrowned side of each crepe. Roll up and place in baking dish seam side down. Repeat with remaining crepes. Top with dollops of sour cream. Bake for 15 minutes or until crepes are heated through. Garnish with parsley sprigs and more sour cream.

# Orange Crêpes

Makes 6 to 8 servings

1¼ cups all-purpose flour
1 tablespoon sugar
¼ teaspoon salt
3 eggs, lightly beaten
1 cup milk
¾ cup water
2 tablespoons Grand Marnier, brandy, *or* orange marmalade
3 tablespoons butter, melted

In a large mixing bowl, stir together flour, sugar, and salt. Add eggs, milk, water, Grand Marnier, and melted butter; stir until blended. Set aside for 30 minutes or store in the refrigerator for several hours. Just before using, bring batter to the consistency of heavy cream by blending in water, 2 tablespoons at a time, if needed. Generously butter a 5 or 6-inch crepe pan. Heat pan until butter sizzles. Ladle about ¼ cup of the batter into pan while tilting the pan so that batter covers the bottom. When batter sets, turn crepe and lightly brown the other side. Turn out onto a paper towel. Repeat with remaining batter, adding butter as necessary.

# Orange Butter

½ cup butter
½ cup powdered sugar
3 tablespoons grated orange peel
2 teaspoons lemon juice
2 tablespoons Grand Marnier *or* brandy

In a mixing bowl, blend butter, sugar, orange peel, lemon juice, and Grand Marnier. Butter each crepe with this mixture. Fold crepes into quarters. In a large, buttered skillet over low heat, warm crepes to serving temperature. Sprinkle with powdered sugar.

# Pasta & Rice

## Stuffed Giant Pasta Shells

Makes 6 servings

- **1 8-ounce package giant pasta shells**
- **3 tablespoons butter**
- **3 tablespoons all-purpose flour**
- **2 cups half-and-half *or* milk**
- **½ pound Gruyere cheese, shredded**
- **½ teaspoon nutmeg**
- **½ teaspoon salt**
- **2 egg yolks**
- **4 tablespoons melted butter**
- **½ cup grated Parmesan cheese**

Preheat oven to 400° F. Grease a 9 x 13-inch baking dish. Cook pasta according to package directions; drain and set aside. In a saucepan over medium heat, melt butter. Stir in flour. Add half-and-half; cook, stirring constantly, until mixture thickens. Stir in Gruyere cheese, nutmeg, and salt. Cook, stirring constantly, until cheese melts. Blend in egg yolks. Fill pasta shells with cheese mixture. Place in a baking dish filling side up. Drizzle with melted butter; sprinkle with Parmesan cheese. Bake for 15 minutes or until heated through.

# Beet Pasta with Basil Sauce

Makes 4 servings

- ½ cup all-purpose flour
- ½ cup quick-mixing flour
- 2 tablespoons pureed canned beets *or* baby-food beets
- ½ teaspoon salt
- 2 eggs
- 2 teaspoons olive oil

In a food processor, combine flours, beets, and salt until well blended. Add eggs and olive oil; blend well. Wrap dough in aluminum foil and allow to rest at room temperature for 30 minutes. Knead dough lightly on a floured surface for 1 minute. Divide dough into quarters. Roll each quarter through a pasta machine using wide noodle cutters, keeping unused dough wrapped in aluminum foil. Place noodles on a pasta holder to dry, about 30 minutes.

- 2 tablespoons cider vinegar
- 2 tablespoons vegetable oil

Bring 4 quarts water to a boil. Add vinegar and vegetable oil. Add noodles and cook just until tender, about 1 minute. Drain noodles and transfer to a heated serving platter. Drizzle Basil Sauce over noodles; toss. Serve immediately.

## Basil Sauce

- 6 tablespoons butter
- 2 tablespoons basil
- ½ teaspoon salt
- ½ teaspoon pepper

Melt butter in small saucepan. Stir in basil, salt, and pepper. Cook over low heat 3 minutes. Keep warm while cooking pasta.

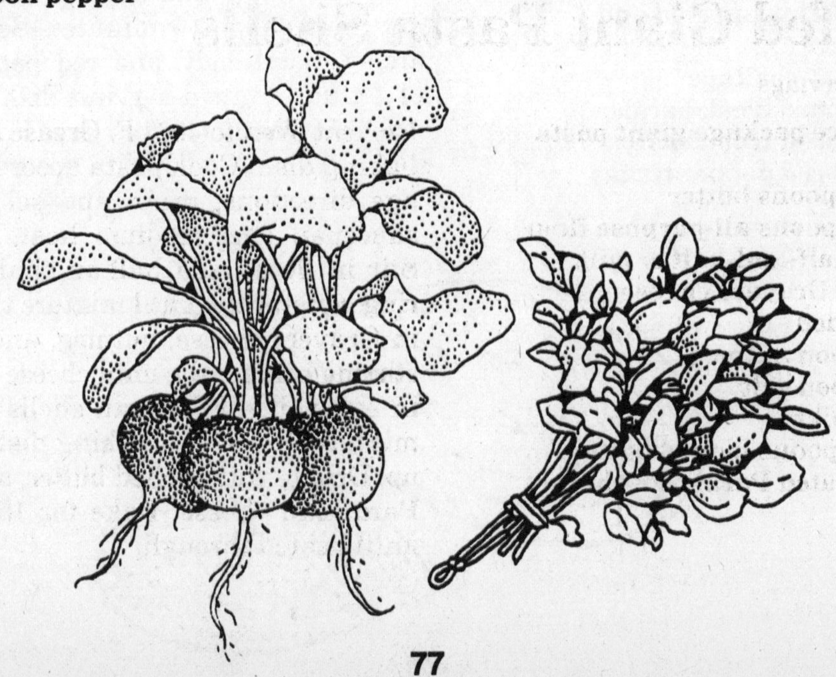

# Pine Nut Pilaf

Makes 4 servings

- 1 tablespoon olive oil *or* vegetable oil
- 1 medium red onion, minced
- 2 to 3 garlic cloves, minced
- 1¼ cups long-grain rice
- ⅓ cup pine nuts *or* slivered almonds
- 2¼ cup chicken broth
- ¼ cup lemon juice
- 1 to 2 tablespoons chopped fresh mint
- Freshly grated rind of 1 lemon
- Freshly ground pepper

Heat oil in a medium saucepan over medium-high heat. Add onion and garlic; sauté until soft, about 5 minutes. Add rice and nuts; stir until golden brown. Add broth and lemon juice; bring to a boil. Reduce heat; cover and simmer until liquid is absorbed, 20 to 25 minutes. Just before serving, add mint, lemon rind, and pepper; fluff with two forks.

# Seafood Fettuccine

**Makes 8 servings**

- **1 12-ounce package fettuccine**
- **¾ pound butter**
- **6 cloves garlic, minced**
- **1 large onion, chopped**
- **1 pound shrimp, peeled and deveined**
- **1 pound bay scallops**
- **½ cup chopped fresh parsley**
- **¼ cup chopped fresh basil**
- **Salt and red pepper flakes to taste**

**Cook fettuccine according to package directions; drain. In a large, heavy skillet, melt butter. Add garlic and onion; sauté until onion is tender. Add shrimp and bay scallops; sauté about 5 minutes. Season with parsley, basil, salt, and red pepper. Place hot fettuccine in a serving dish. Add seafood. Toss gently to mix. Serve immediately.**

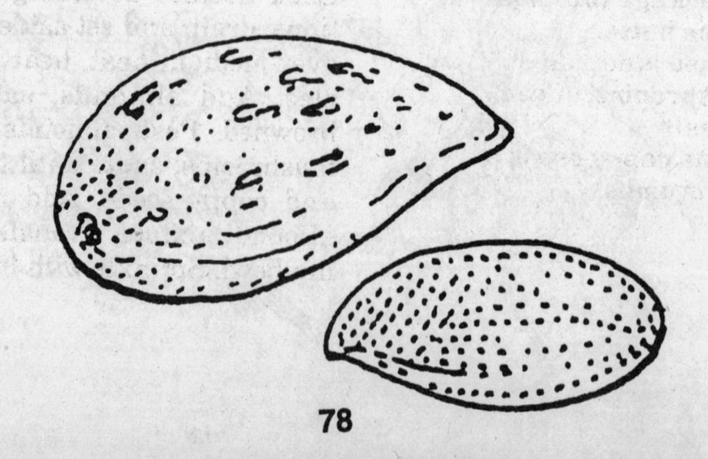

# Pasta with Goat Cheese

Makes 8 servings

- 1 16-ounce package thin pasta
- 5 tablespoons butter
- 2 large red bell peppers, thinly sliced
- 1 medium red onion, thinly sliced
- 1½ cups light cream
- 1 tablespoon basil
- 6 ounces shredded goat cheese
- 1 cup chopped pecans

Cook pasta according to package directions; drain. In a heavy skillet over medium heat, heat 2 tablespoons of the butter. Add peppers and onion; sauté until vegetables are tender, about 3 minutes. Transfer vegetables to a mixing bowl. In a small saucepan, heat cream to just below a simmer. Add hot cream to vegetables along with basil and goat cheese. Toss gently. Transfer hot pasta to a serving bowl. Add remaining butter, vegetable-cheese mixture, and pecans; toss to mix. Serve immediately.

# Noodles and Almonds

Makes 6 servings

- 1 8-ounce package thin noodles
- 5 tablespoons butter
- ¾ cup blanched almonds
- ½ pound mushrooms, sliced
- ¼ teaspoon salt
- 4 tablespoons poppy seeds
- ½ cup bread crumbs

Cook noodles according to package directions; drain and set aside. In a large skillet over medium heat, heat butter until it sizzles. Add almonds; sauté until lightly browned. Push almonds to one side. Add mushrooms; sauté until tender. Stir in salt and poppy seeds. Add noodles; toss with almond mixture. Transfer pasta to a serving bowl. Sprinkle with bread crumbs.

# Stir-Fry Pasta Primavera

Makes 4 servings

- 1/2 cup unsalted butter
- 1 medium onion, minced
- 2 large cloves garlic, minced
- 1 pound asparagus, cut diagonally in 1/4-inch slices, tips intact
- 1/2 pound cauliflower, broken up
- 1/2 pound mushrooms, sliced
- 1 zucchini, cut in 1/4-inch slices
- 1 small carrot, halved lengthwise and cut in 1/8-inch slices
- 1/2 cup chicken broth
- 1/4 cup dry white wine
- 1 teaspoon dried basil leaves
- 1/2 teaspoon oregano leaves
- 1 cup frozen early peas, thawed
- 5 green onions, chopped
- 2 tablespoons minced parsley
- Salt and pepper to taste
- 1 pound linguine, cooked and drained
- 1/2 cup grated Parmesan cheese

Heat wok or large, deep skillet over medium-high heat. Add butter, onion, and garlic; stir-fry until onion is tender, about 2 minutes. Stir in asparagus, cauliflower, mushrooms, zucchini, and carrot; stir-fry 2 minutes. Increase heat to high. Add broth, wine, basil, and oregano. Bring to a boil; boil until liquid is slightly reduced, about 3 minutes. Add peas and green onions; heat through, stirring gently, for 1 minute. Add parsley, salt, and pepper. Add pasta and cheese; toss until cheese is evenly distributed and pasta is heated through.

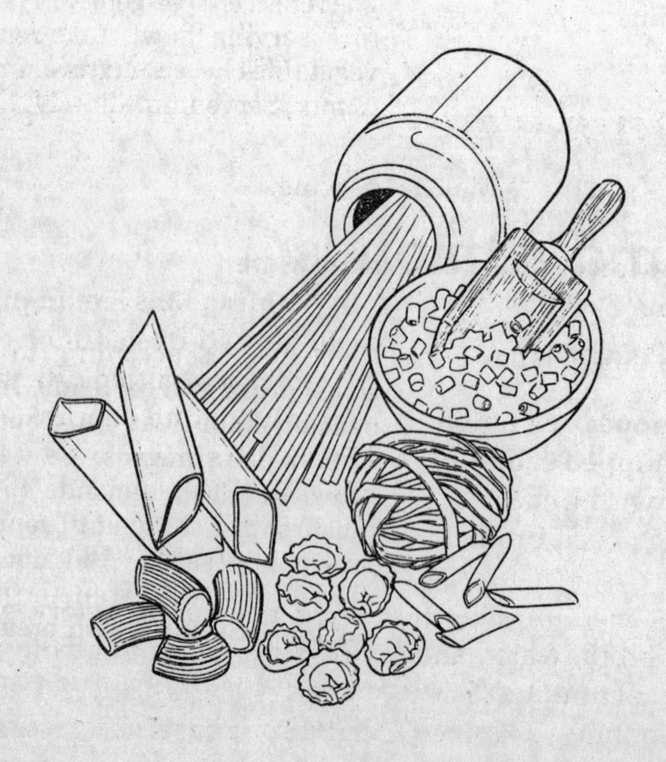

# Little Shells with Ham and Cheese

Makes 6 servings

- 1 8-ounce package small pasta shells
- 3 tablespoons butter at room temperature
- 1 cup ricotta cheese
- 1 8-ounce package cream cheese at room temperature
- ½ teaspoon tarragon
- Salt and pepper to taste
- 8 ounces cooked ham, shredded

Cook pasta shells according to package directions; drain and set aside. In a deep bowl, blend butter, ricotta cheese, and cream cheese. Add tarragon, salt, and pepper; beat mixture until light and fluffy. Stir in ham. Toss cheese mixture with hot pasta.

# Lemon-Dill Rice

Makes 4 servings

- 1 tablespoon safflower oil *or* vegetable oil
- 1 cup long-grain brown *or* white rice
- 1 cup finely chopped red onion
- 1 stalk finely chopped celery
- 1 large garlic clove, minced
- 1 13-ounce can chicken broth
- ⅓ cup water
- 1 to 2 tablespoons lemon juice
- ¼ cup minced fresh dill *or* 1 tablespoon dried dill
- Freshly ground pepper
- Fresh dill sprigs
- Lemon slices

Heat safflower oil over medium-high heat. Add rice, onion, celery, and garlic; sauté about 5 minutes. Add broth, water, and lemon juice. Bring to a boil; reduce heat and simmer, covered, 20 to 30 minutes. Stir in minced dill and pepper. Remove from heat. Cover and let stand 10 minutes. Garnish with dill sprigs and lemon slices.

# Pasta with Garlic

Makes 4 servings

- 2 cups chicken broth
- 2 cups water
- 1/2 pound fresh pasta
- 1 tablespoon butter *or* margarine
- 2 cloves garlic, minced
- 1/4 cup minced fresh parsley
- 1 teaspoon basil, marjoram, oregano, *or* thyme
- Freshly grated Parmesan, Romano, *or* Sapsago cheese

Bring broth and water to a boil in a large pot. Add pasta and cook until tender but still firm, 4 to 6 minutes. Drain and transfer to a heated platter. Melt butter *or* margarine in a small saucepan and stir in garlic, parsley, and herbs. Heat gently. Pour parsley mixture over noodles and toss to coat well. Garnish with grated cheese.

# Pasta with Artichoke Hearts

Makes 6 servings

- 3/4 pound spaghetti
- 2 9-ounce packages frozen artichoke hearts
- 4 tablespoons vegetable oil
- 1 onion, thinly sliced
- 4 large tomatoes, peeled and chopped
- 1/2 teaspoon salt
- 1/2 teaspoon pepper
- 1/2 teaspoon garlic powder
- 1/4 cup chopped fresh parsley

Cook spaghetti according to package directions; drain and set aside. Cook artichoke hearts according to package directions; set aside. In a large skillet, heat oil. Add onion; sauté until tender. Stir in artichoke hearts; sauté for 2 minutes. Stir in tomatoes, salt, pepper, and garlic powder. Divide spaghetti among 6 plates. Top with artichoke heart sauce; sprinkle with parsley.

# Pasta and Pea Pods

Makes 4 servings

8 ounces mostaccioli
1 6-ounce package frozen pea pods
½ cup butter *or* margarine
Salt and pepper to taste
¼ cup grated Romano cheese
Julienned carrots, optional

Cook mostaccioli and pea pods according to package directions; drain and keep warm. In a skillet melt butter *or* margarine over medium heat until golden brown. Remove from heat; add mostaccioli and pea pods. Toss together. Season to taste with salt and pepper. Transfer to a serving bowl; sprinkle with Romano cheese. Garnish with julienned carrots, if desired.

# Pesto Sauce

Makes 6 servings

1 cup fresh basil leaves
4 cloves garlic, minced
¼ cup pine nuts
¼ cup olive oil
½ cup grated Parmesan cheese
½ teaspoon salt

In a blender or a food processor, puree all ingredients until the consistency of a thick puree. Drizzle room temperature sauce over piping hot cooked pasta.

# Turkey Tetrazzini

Makes 6 servings

**1 8-ounce package thin spaghetti**
**½ cup butter**
**1 large onion, minced**
**1 pound mushrooms, sliced**
**1½ pounds cooked turkey breast, cubed**
**4 tablespoons all-purpose flour**
**1½ cups chicken stock**
**Salt and pepper to taste**
**1 cup half-and-half**

Preheat oven to 350° F. Butter a 9 x 13-inch baking dish. Cook spaghetti according to package directions; drain and set aside. In a large, heavy skillet over medium heat, heat half of the butter until it sizzles. Add onion and mushrooms; sauté until tender. Stir in turkey. In a separate saucepan over medium heat, melt remaining butter. Blend in flour. Add chicken stock, salt, and pepper. Cook, stirring constantly, until mixture thickens. Blend in half-and-half. Stir sauce into vegetables and turkey. Add spaghetti; toss to mix. Transfer to prepared baking dish. Bake for 10 minutes or until heated through.

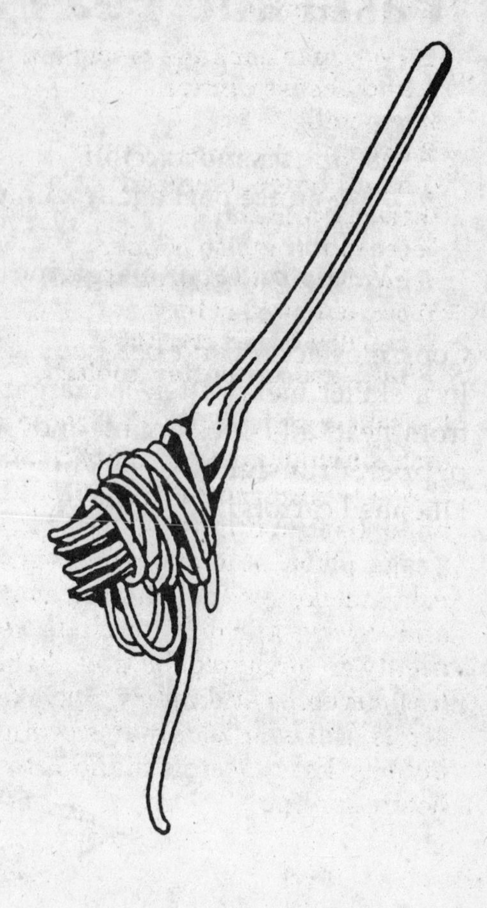

# Rosemary Macaroni

Makes 4 servings

**2 quarts water**
**½ teaspoon salt**
**8 ounces elbow macaroni (whole wheat, yellow, and/or green)**
**1 tablespoon oil**
**1 teaspoon lemon juice**
**Chopped fresh rosemary *or* chives**

Bring water and salt to a boil. Add macaroni, oil, and lemon juice and cook until tender but firm. Add rosemary and toss before serving.

# Easy Macaroni Egg Bake

Makes 6 servings

**1 7¼-ounce package macaroni and cheese dinner**
**¾ cup milk**
**2 eggs**
**1 small onion, chopped**
**½ teaspoon salt**
**¼ teaspoon white pepper**
**6 hard-boiled eggs, chopped**
**½ cup chopped celery**
**¼ cup dry bread crumbs**
**3 tablespoons butter, melted**

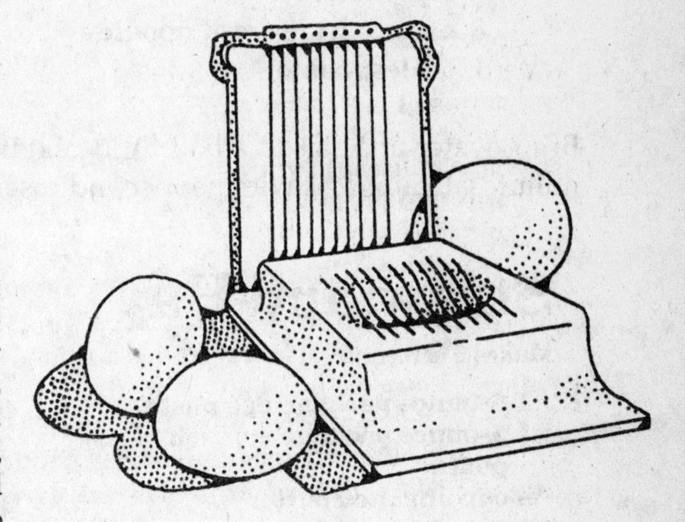

Preheat oven to 350° F. Grease an 11 x 7-inch baking dish. Prepare macaroni and cheese dinner according to package directions. In a mixing bowl, beat together milk, 2 eggs, onion, salt, and pepper until blended. Add macaroni and cheese, chopped eggs, and celery; stir until well mixed. Spread evenly in prepared baking dish. Combine bread crumbs and butter. Sprinkle over casserole. Bake for 20 minutes or until hot and bubbly. Let casserole stand 3 to 5 minutes before serving.

# Oranged Borscht

Makes 4 servings

**1 pound cooked beets, sliced**
**1 14½-ounce can low-sodium chicken broth**
**¼ cup coarsely chopped red onion**
**1 clove garlic**
**3 to 4 tablespoons orange juice**
**½ cup plain yogurt *or* Neufchatel cheese, softened**
**1 cucumber, peeled and diced**
**Orange slices**

Process or blend first 5 ingredients until smooth. Stir in yogurt and cucumber. Chill and garnish with orange slices before serving.

# Fresh Herbed Pasta

Makes 4 servings

- 2 quarts water
- 1 teaspoon salt
- 8 ounces wide fresh noodles
- 1 tablespoon oil
- Freshly ground black pepper
- 2 tablespoons chopped fresh rosemary, thyme, *or* chives

Bring water and salt to a boil. Add noodles and oil; cook until tender but firm, 5 to 8 minutes. Drain. Toss with pepper and rosemary before serving.

# Straw and Hay

Makes 6 servings

- **1 8-ounce package egg pasta**
- **1 8-ounce package spinach pasta**
- **½ cup unsalted butter**
- **1½ cups heavy cream**
- **½ teaspoon salt**
- **½ teaspoon pepper**
- **1¼ cups grated Parmesan cheese**

**Cook egg pasta and spinach pasta separately according to package directions; drain and set aside. In a large, heavy skillet over medium heat, melt butter. Stir in cream; cook, stirring constantly, until mixture thickens slightly. Season with salt and pepper. Toss egg pasta and spinach pasta together. Divide pasta among 6 deep soup bowls. Drizzle sauce over pasta. Sprinkle with Parmesan cheese.**

## Parmesan Pinwheels

Makes 4 servings

- **1 cup butter *or* margarine**
- **1 cup flour**
- **1/2 cup shredded sharp Meunster *or* sharp Brick cheese**
- **1/2 cup sour cream**
- **2/3 cup freshly grated Parmesan *or* Romano cheese**
- **1/2 teaspoon cayenne pepper**
- **1/2 teaspoon paprika**
- **1/4 teaspoon salt**
- **1/4 teaspoon Tabasco sauce**
- **Fresh-cut vegetables *or* fruit, optional**

Using a pastry blender, cut together butter *or* margarine and flour. Blend in Meunster cheese and sour cream. Divide dough into 4 parts; wrap and chill for 15 minutes. Combine Parmesan, pepper, paprika, salt, and Tabasco sauce; set aside. On a floured surface roll one part of pastry into a 12 x 6-inch rectangle. Sprinkle with 2 tablespoons of the Parmesan mixture. Fold in 6-inch sides to meet in center, forming a square. Sprinkle with 1 tablespoon of the Parmesan mixture. Fold lengthwise again. On folded edge make 1/4-inch cuts, 1 inch apart. Bring ends together, forming a wheel, and place on ungreased baking sheet. Repeat with remaining pastry sections. Bake 10 to 15 minutes at 450° or until golden brown. Serve with vegetables *or* fruit, if desired.

# Chicago Style Open-Face

Makes 6 sandwiches

**6 slices rye bread**
**½ head iceberg lettuce, cut into 6 portions**
**6 slices Swiss cheese**
**12 ounces sliced turkey *or* chicken**
**6 slices cooked bacon, halved**
**1 large tomato, cut into 6 slices**

On each slice of bread, place a wedge of lettuce; top with a slice of Swiss cheese. Distribute turkey among the 6 sandwiches. Drizzle sandwiches with Zesty Dressing. Cross 2 bacon strips over each sandwich; top with a tomato slice.

# Zesty Dressing

**2 cups mayonnaise**
**4 tablespoons chili sauce**
**4 tablespoons chopped sweet pickle**
**1 small red onion, minced**

In a deep bowl, stir together all ingredients until well mixed. Cover and chill until ready to serve.

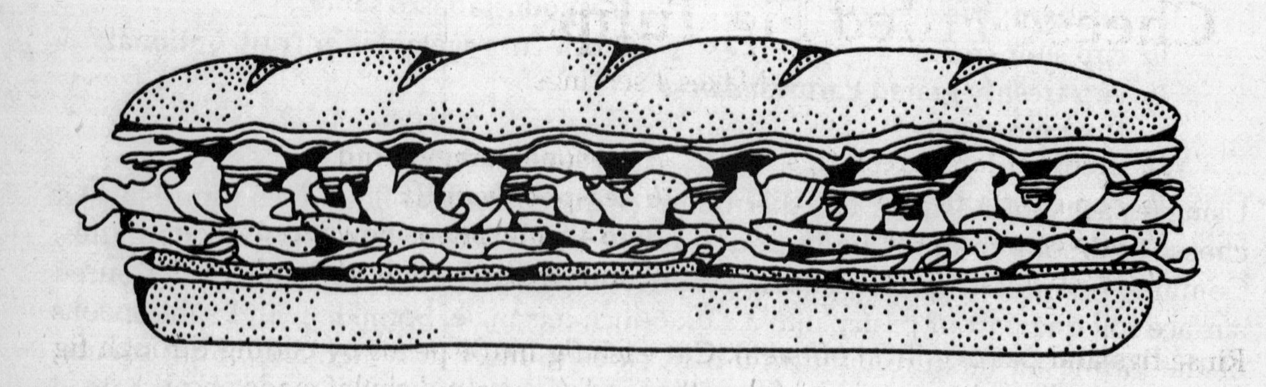

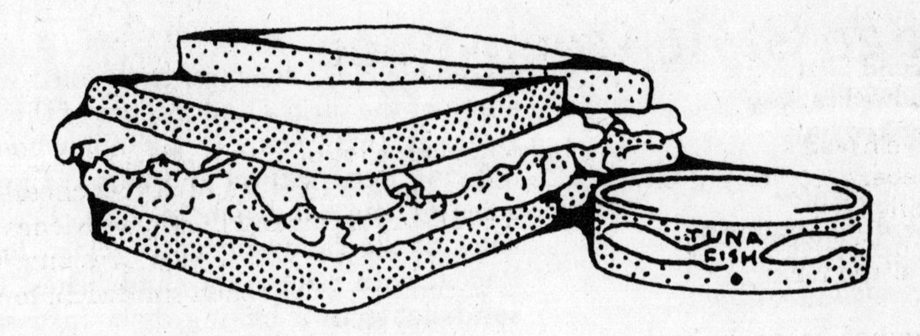


# Tuna Salad Filling

Makes 3 cups

**2 7½-ounce cans tuna, drained**
**2 hard-boiled eggs, chopped**
**1 small red onion, thinly sliced**
**½ cup chopped celery**
**½ cup mayonnaise**
**½ teaspoon salt**
**½ teaspoon garlic powder**
**¼ teaspoon pepper**

In a large mixing bowl, flake tuna. Add remaining ingredients; toss to mix. Cover with plastic wrap and refrigerate until ready to serve. Good on dark rolls or white toast, or as a stuffing for tomatoes.

# Cheese-Filled Fig Tulips

Makes 4 servings

**12 medium-large fresh figs**
**½ cup ricotta cheese**
**½ cup cream cheese**
**½ teaspoon lemon rind**
**½ teaspoon orange rind**
**½ teaspoon vanilla**
**3 to 4 tablespoons powdered sugar**
**12 unblanched whole almonds**

Rinse figs and pat dry. Trim off stem. Cut each fig into 4 petals by cutting through fig from stem end to within ½ inch of the other end. (Cover and chill if made ahead.)

Process or blend remaining ingredients except almonds. Stand 2 to 3 figs upright on each plate. Gently open each fig and spoon in about 2 tablespoons of cheese mixture. Top each with an almond.

# Broiled Monte Cristo

Makes 3 sandwiches

6 slices bread
6 slices cooked turkey
6 slices cooked ham
3 eggs
2 tablespoons water
2 tablespoons vegetable oil
1 tablespoon butter
1½ cups shredded provolone cheese
½ cup milk
½ cup mayonnaise
⅛ teaspoon nutmeg
Parsley
Lemon slices

Assemble 3 sandwiches, each filled with 2 slices of the turkey and 2 slices of the ham. Beat eggs with water in a shallow bowl. In a frying pan, heat oil and butter. Dip both sides of one sandwich in eggs. Fry both sides of the sandwich until golden brown. Repeat with remaining sandwiches. Place sandwiches in a baking dish. In a saucepan, combine cheese, milk, mayonnaise, and nutmeg. Heat, stirring constantly, until cheese melts and mixture is smooth. Pour over sandwiches. Broil 6 inches from heat for 5 minutes or until bubbly. Garnish with parsley and lemon slices.

# Barbecued Beef on Buns

Makes 6 sandwiches

1½ pounds ground beef
1 onion, thinly sliced
Salt and pepper to taste
1 cup catsup
1 tablespoon mustard
3 tablespoons brown sugar
2 tablespoons red wine vinegar
1 teaspoon Worcestershire sauce
6 hamburger buns, split

In a large skillet over medium heat, sauté hamburger and onion until hamburger is browned and onion is tender. Pour off excess fat. Add remaining ingredients. Cook and stir until mixture simmers. Toast hamburger buns. Fill with meat mixture.

# Hot Roast Beef Sandwiches

Makes 8 sandwiches

**¼ cup butter**
**1 large red onion, thinly sliced**
**1 pound mushrooms, sliced**
**½ cup dry sherry**
**1 bouillon cube, dissolved in ½ cup hot water**
**1 teaspoon fresh lemon juice**
**1 teaspoon Worcestershire sauce**
**2½ pounds sirloin tip roast, cooked and thinly sliced**
**8 party rolls or pita breads**

In a large, heavy skillet over medium heat, heat butter until it sizzles. Add onion; sauté until tender. Add mushrooms; sauté briefly. Stir in sherry, bouillon, lemon juice, and Worcestershire sauce; simmer 5 minutes. Push vegetables to side of pan; add sliced beef. Spoon vegetables and sauce over beef. Cover pan; simmer until beef is hot. Warm the rolls; split and fill with beef and vegetables.

# Chicken Sandwiches Veronique

Makes 12 sandwiches

**3½ cups cubed cooked chicken**
**1 cup chopped celery**
**¾ cup seedless grapes, halved**
**½ cup chopped pecans**
**¼ cup coconut flakes**
**¾ cup mayonnaise**
**½ teaspoon curry powder (optional)**
**Salt and pepper to taste**
**¼ cup heavy cream, whipped**
**12 croissants**
**Lettuce leaves**
**Tomato slices**

In a large mixing bowl, stir together chicken, celery, grapes, pecans, and coconut. In a separate bowl, combine mayonnaise, curry powder, salt, and pepper; fold into whipped cream. Fold chicken mixture gently into whipped cream mixture. Cover and chill. Slice open croissants; line openings with lettuce leaves and tomato slices. Fill with chicken mixture.

# Caviar and Olive Toast Rounds

Makes 4 servings

- 1/4 cup caviar
- 10 to 12 stuffed green olives, finely chopped
- 2 to 3 tablespoons lemon juice
- 1 to 2 tablespoon minced red onion
- Melba toast rounds
- 3 hard-boiled egg yolks, sieved

Mix first 4 ingredients. Spread on toast rounds and sprinkle with sieved yolks.

# Cheese and Apple Wafers

Makes 4 servings

- 1 cup flour
- 1 1/4 cup grated Cheddar cheese
- 1/4 pound butter *or* margarine
- 1 teaspoon Worcestershire sauce
- Minced chives, cilantro, *or* parsley
- Poppy, caraway, *or* sesame seeds
- Apple *or* pear wedges

Combine flour and cheese; cut in butter *or* margarine. Add sauce and blend well. Roll dough into long strips about 3/4 inch in diameter. Freeze 15 minutes. Slice into thin wafers. Bake at 475° for 10 minutes on greased cookie sheet. Sprinkle wafers with different combinations of minced chives, cilantro, *or* parsley; poppy, caraway, *or* sesame seeds. Serve with apple wedges.

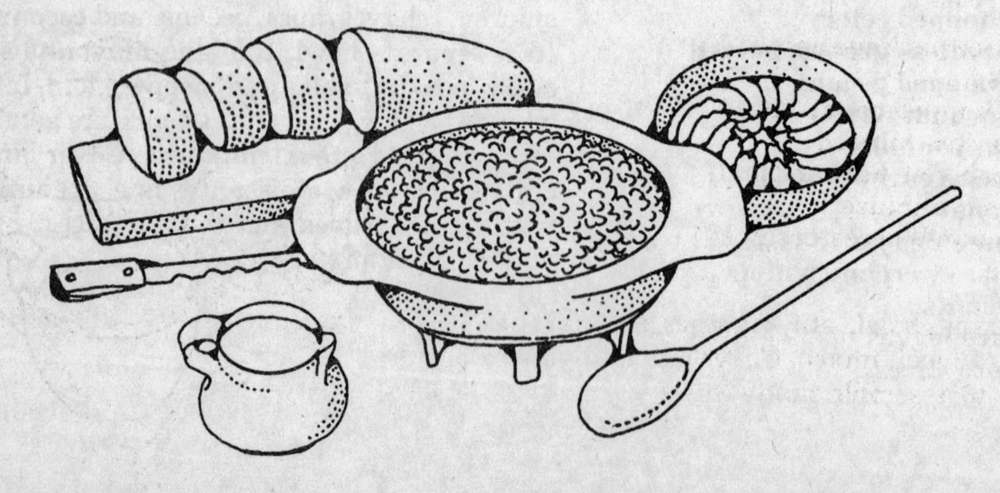

# Sardine Cornucopias

Makes 12 sandwiches

**12 slices dark sandwich bread**
**2 2¾-ounce cans sardines, drained**
**4 hard-boiled eggs, chopped**
**1 tablespoon lemon juice**
**Butter**

Cut crusts from bread. In a mixing bowl, combine remaining ingredients until well mixed. Spread bread slices with filling. Bring opposite corners of bread together to form a triangle. Spread edges of bread with butter; press together. Secure with a wooden pick. Cover sandwiches with a damp cloth; refrigerate at least 1 hour. Remove toothpicks before serving.

# Beef and Cream Cheese Filling

Makes 1½ cups

**1 8-ounce package cream cheese**
**½ cup chopped cooked beef**
**1 red onion, minced**
**3 tablespoons half-and-half**
**¼ cup mayonnaise**
**¼ teaspoon Worcestershire sauce**

In a mixing bowl, stir together all ingredients until well mixed. Cover and chill until ready to assemble sandwiches.

# Turkey Salad Filling

Makes 7 cups

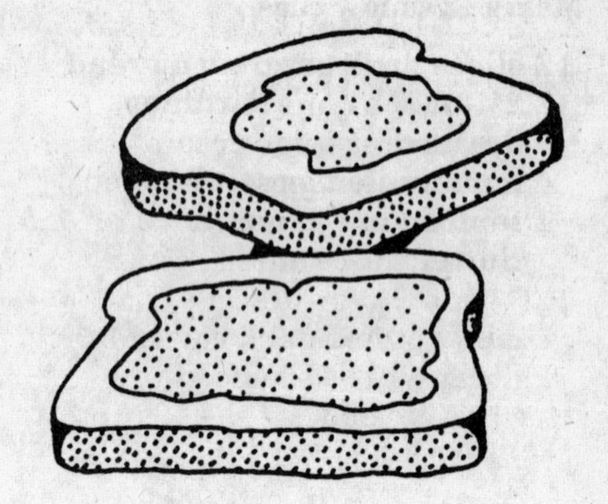

2½ cups diced cooked chicken
2 cups chopped celery
¾ cup toasted almonds, chopped
Salt and pepper to taste
½ teaspoon celery seed
½ teaspoon garlic powder
1 cup mayonnaise
1 tablespoon fresh lemon juice
1 red bell pepper, chopped

In a mixing bowl, stir together all ingredients until well blended. Adjust seasonings. Cover and chill until ready to assemble sandwiches.

# Orange Date Tea Sandwiches

Makes 6 sandwiches

1 large orange, peeled and segmented
1 8-ounce package cream cheese at room temperature
½ cup pitted chopped dates
1 16-ounce can brown bread
Butter at room temperature

Cut orange segments into small pieces. In a mixing bowl, stir together cream cheese, dates, and orange pieces. Slice brown bread into 12 slices. Butter slices; spread 6 slices with filling. Top with remaining slices. Place sandwiches on a serving tray, cover with plastic wrap, and chill until ready to serve.

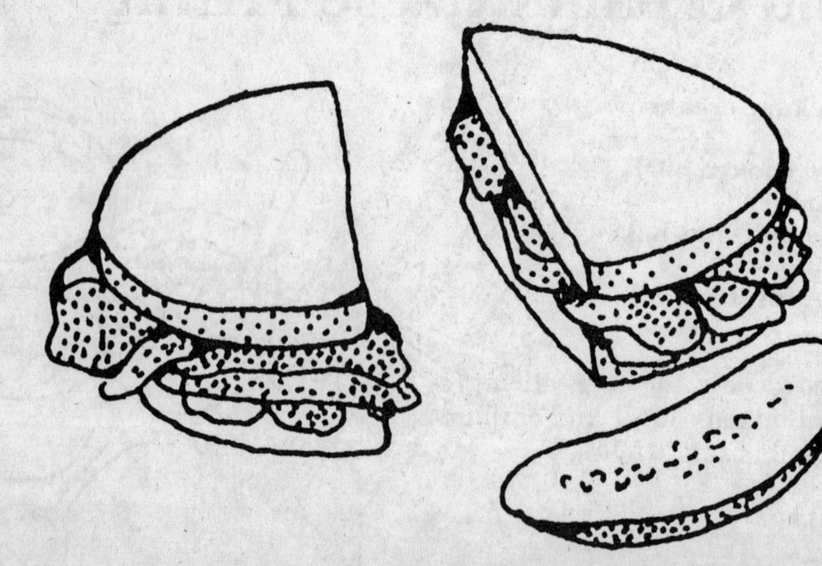

# Cream Cheese Fruit Sandwiches

Makes 8 small sandwiches

**1 8-ounce package cream cheese at room temperature**
**1 8-ounce can crushed pineapple, drained**
**½ teaspoon vanilla**
**¼ cup chopped dark red cherries**
**8 slices white *or* whole wheat bread**

In a mixing bowl, stir together cream cheese, pineapple, and vanilla until well mixed. Stir in cherries. Assemble 4 sandwiches. With cookie cutters or a sharp knife, cut sandwiches into desired shapes.

# Asparagus Roll-Ups

Makes 12 sandwiches

**12 slices fresh white bread, crusts removed**
**1 8-ounce package cream cheese at room temperature**
**4 tablespoons sour cream**
**1 10-ounce package frozen asparagus spears, cooked**
**Melted butter**
**Nutmeg**

Preheat broiler. Flatten each slice of bread with a rolling pin. In a small bowl, stir together cream cheese and sour cream until well blended. Spread cheese mixture on bread. Place an asparagus spear on each slice of bread. Roll up jelly roll style. Place seam side down on a baking sheet. Brush with melted butter. Sprinkle lightly with nutmeg. Bake, turning once, until lightly browned.

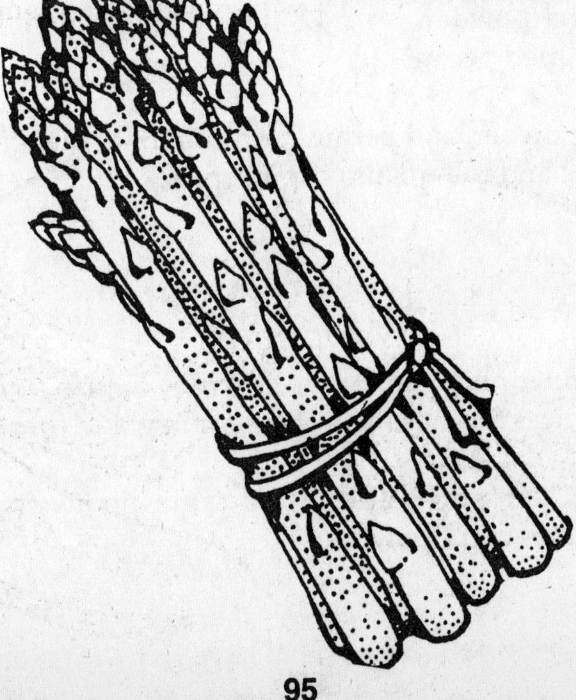

# Egg and Cheese Spread

Makes 4 cups

- 6 hard-boiled eggs, chopped
- ¾ cup grated Cheddar cheese
- ¼ cup chopped pecans
- 1 tablespoon chopped pimiento
- ½ cup mayonnaise

In a mixing bowl, blend together all ingredients until mixture is of spreading consistency. Excellent for sandwiches or as a stuffing for celery stalks.

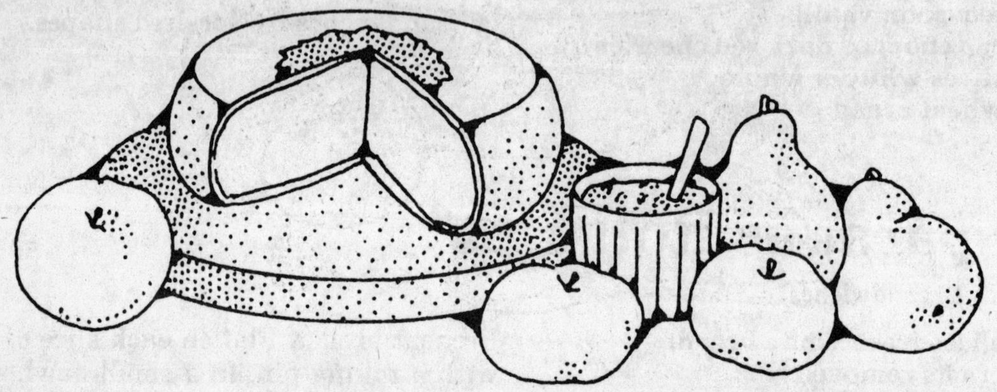

# Cornucopia Roll-Ups

Makes 4 servings

- 1 3-ounce package cream cheese
- 1 tablespoon curry powder
- ½ cup finely chopped pecans
- 2 to 3 tablespoons milk
- Freshly ground black pepper to taste
- 12 turkey luncheon meat slices

Combine cheese, curry powder, and pecans. Stir in milk to moisten and season to taste. Spread over turkey slices and roll up into cornucopias.

## Variations

**Pineapple-Yogurt Cornucopias:** Substitute 1/2 cup yogurt, 1/4 cup drained crushed pineapple, and 12 ham slices for the cream cheese, curry, and turkey.

**Ham Rolls:** Substitute ham slices and 2 to 3 tablespoons finely chopped ginger preserves for the turkey and curry powder.

# Soups & Salads

## Spinach Salad with Lemon-Lime Vinaigrette

Makes 4 servings

- **1 bunch spinach, stems removed**
- **3 green onions, sliced**
- **½ cup sliced radishes**
- **1 cup bean sprouts, optional**
- **6 to 8 cherry tomatoes, halved**
- **Lemon-Lime Vinaigrette (below)**

Tear spinach into bite-size pieces. Arrange other vegetables in groups on top of spinach. Serve with Lemon-Lime Vinaigrette.

### Lemon-Lime Vinaigrette

Makes 1 cup

- **¼ cup safflower oil**
- **2 tablespoons lemon juice**
- **2 tablespoons lime juice**
- **2 tablespoons minced parsley**

Combine all ingredients; mix well.

# Sunny Fruit Salad

Makes 4 servings

- **2 small head Bibb *or* butterhead lettuce**
- **1/2 avocado, sliced**
- **1 nectarine, peeled and sliced into rounds**
- **1/2 grapefruit, peeled and sliced into rounds**
- **1 orange, peeled and sliced into rounds**
- **Ginger Dressing (below)**

Separate lettuce into leaves. Arrange avocado, nectarine, grapefruit, and orange slices attractively over lettuce. Top with Ginger Dressing.

*Note:* Slices of peaches and papaya may be substituted for the nectarine, grapefruit, *or* orange.

## Ginger Dressing

Makes 1 cup

- **1 cup plain yogurt**
- **1/4 cup orange juice**
- **Sugar to taste**
- **1/2 teaspoon minced fresh ginger**

Stir all ingredients together. Let dressing stand at least 5 minutes before serving to blend flavors.

### Variation

Omit minced ginger and add 2 teaspoons grated orange peel and a dash of ground cloves.

# Sherried Endive Salad

Makes 4 servings

- **12 medium *or* 8 large mushrooms, trimmed**
- **2 heads endive *or* escarole, torn**
- **2 green onions, chopped**
- **½ cup plain yogurt**
- **1½ teaspoons Dijon-style mustard**
- **1 to 2 tablespoons dry sherry**

Arrange mushrooms on endive *or* escarole. Mix together remaining ingredients and spoon half of dressing over salad. Serve balance of dressing on the side.

# Italian Tomato Cucumber Salad

Makes 4 servings

- **5 or 6 Italian-style plum tomatoes *or* 3 large ripe tomatoes**
- **1 stalk celery, thinly sliced**
- **1 cucumber, sliced**
- **3 or 4 red onions, sliced**
- **1 clove garlic, halved**
- **Black peppercorn**
- **Chopped fresh oregano**
- **Minced fresh basil**
- **2 tablespoons olive oil *or* vegetable oil**
- **2 tablespoons red wine vinegar**

Cut tomatoes into wedges and combine with celery, cucumber, and onion. Rub a glass serving bowl with cut side of garlic; add vegetables. Grind pepper over all and season generously with oregano and basil. Drizzle oil and vinegar evenly over salad; toss gently. Serve at room temperature.

# Grilled Cheese and Walnut Salad with Mango Dressing

Makes 4 servings

**1 head radicchio**
**1 head butter lettuce**
**1 head Arugula**
**4 to 6 ounces mild herbed goat cheese**
**½ cup walnut *or* hazelnut oil *or* vegetable oil**
**1 tablespoon mango chutney**
**1 tablespoon plain yogurt**
**2 teaspoons red wine vinegar**
**1 cup coarsely chopped walnuts**

Discard any outer leaves, then wash and pat dry all greens. Refrigerate. Slice cheese into four chunks. Grill or broil briefly and set aside. Process or blend next 4 ingredients for dressing. Arrange lettuce leaves on a platter. Form a ring of Arugula over lettuce. Place cheese in center. Sprinkle with walnuts and drizzle on dressing.

# Orange Tailgate Salad

Makes 8 to 10 servings

**1 bunch leaf lettuce**
**6 large oranges, peeled and sliced**
**2 bananas, sliced**
**1 avocado, sliced**
**1 pint strawberries**
**3 peaches, cut into chunks**

**Arrange lettuce leaves on a flat platter. Arrange fruit over lettuce.**

## Yogurt Dressing

**1 cup plain yogurt**
**2 teaspoons lime juice**
**Honey to taste**
**Dash salt**
**Lime slices**

**In a small bowl, combine all ingredients except lime slices. Line a serving bowl with lime slices. Spoon in yogurt.**

# Gazpacho Macaroni Salad

Makes 6 to 8 servings

- 2 cups uncooked macaroni
- 1 10-ounce package frozen peas
- 3 medium tomatoes, peeled and chopped
- 1 cup chopped celery
- 1 medium cucumber, diced
- 1 green pepper, chopped
- 5 green onions, thinly sliced
- 6 ounces salami, cubed
- ¼ cup chopped fresh parsley
- ⅓ cup olive oil
- ¼ cup wine vinegar
- 1 teaspoon salt
- ½ teaspoon Worcestershire sauce
- Hot pepper sauce to taste
- 1 clove garlic, pressed
- Lettuce cups
- Ripe olives

Cook macaroni according to package directions; drain; rinse in cold water; drain again. Place peas in a bowl; cover with boiling water; let stand 1 to 2 minutes; drain. In a bowl, combine macaroni, peas, tomatoes, celery, cucumber, green pepper, onions, salami, and parsley. In a separate bowl, beat together remaining ingredients until well blended. Pour over macaroni mixture; toss lightly. Serve in lettuce cups; garnish with olives. Note: macaroni and vegetable mixture may be combined with dressing and chilled 3 hours before serving. Toss before spooning into lettuce cups.

# Swiss Cheese Soup

Makes 4 servings

- 3 tablespoons butter *or* margarine
- 1/4 cup flour
- 1 teaspoon instant chicken bouillon granules
- 1/4 teaspoon paprika
- 3 1/2 cup milk
- 6 slices processed Swiss cheese
- 1 teaspoon snipped chives

Melt butter *or* margarine in medium saucepan. Stir in flour, bouillon granules, and paprika. Cook and stir over medium heat until bubbly. Add milk all at once. Cook and stir until thick and bubbly; cook and stir 1 minute more. Stir in cheese and chives. Stir over low heat until cheese melts.

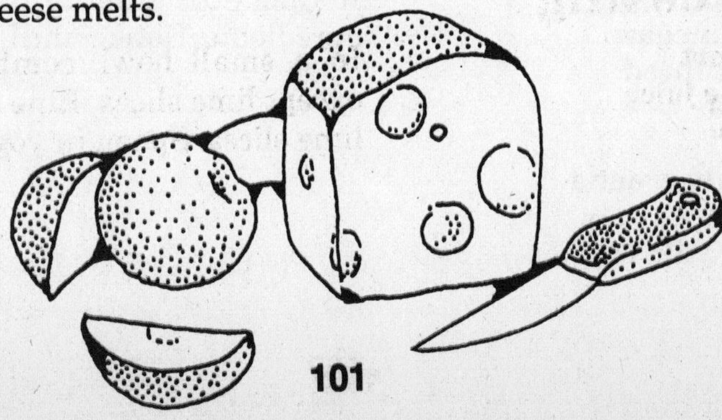

# Fruited Watercress Salad

Makes 4 servings

- 2 oranges, peeled and sliced
- 2 kiwi fruit, peeled and sliced
- 1 grapefruit, peeled and sliced
- 2 bunches watercress, tough stems removed
- 1 head butter lettuce, cleaned and separated into leaves
- Lemon *or* lime juice
- Vegetable oil

Arrange fruit on a bed of watercress and butter lettuce. Sprinkle with juice and oil to taste.

# Salad Nicoise

Makes 6 to 8 servings

- 1 head Boston lettuce
- ¾ pound new potatoes, boiled, peeled, and sliced
- ¾ pound green beans, trimmed, cooked, and drained
- 4 hard-boiled eggs, sliced
- 1 large Bermuda onion, sliced
- 3 large tomatoes, sliced
- 2 green peppers, sliced
- 1 2-ounce can anchovy fillets, drained
- 2 7-ounce cans solid-pack tuna
- 1 cup pitted ripe olives

Tear lettuce into bite-size pieces; arrange on a serving platter. Arrange remaining ingredients attractively over lettuce. Drizzle Basil Vinaigrette over salad. Chill until ready to serve.

# Basil Vinaigrette

- ½ cup corn oil *or* olive oil
- ¼ cup red wine vinegar
- 2 cloves garlic, minced
- 2 teaspoons basil
- ½ teaspoon salt
- ¼ teaspoon freshly ground black pepper

In a jar with a tight-fitting lid, combine all ingredients. Shake until blended.

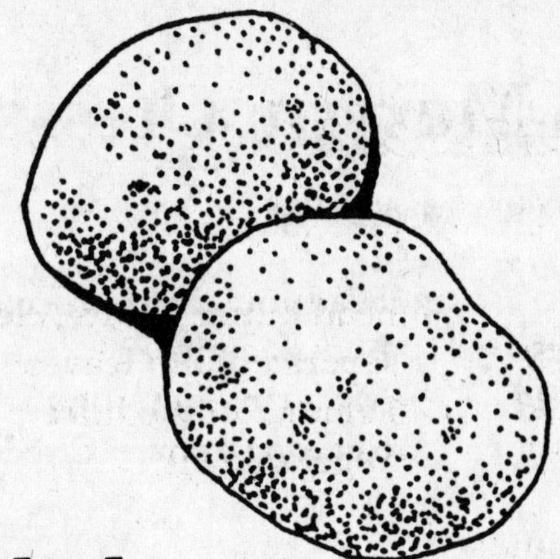

# Potato Salad

Makes 8 servings

2 pounds small red potatoes, cooked and drained
5 tablespoons vegetable oil
3 tablespoons red wine vinegar
2 cloves garlic, minced
Salt and pepper to taste
1 pound Italian sausage, cooked and sliced into ¾-inch pieces
1 onion, thinly sliced
1 red bell pepper, sliced

Slice potatoes and place in a serving bowl. Add oil, vinegar, minced garlic, salt, and pepper; toss gently to coat potatoes. Stir in sausage, onion, and red pepper. Chill until ready to serve.

# Vegetable Salad

Makes 8 servings

½ small cauliflower, broken into flowerets
½ pound green beans
1 16-ounce can kidney beans
1 16-ounce can garbanzos
4 green onions, chopped
1 2¼-ounce can sliced olives
½ cup olive oil
¼ cup wine vinegar
1 teaspoon tarragon
Salt and pepper to taste
1 bunch leaf lettuce
1 head Boston lettuce
3 large tomatoes, sliced
3 hard-boiled eggs, sliced

Blanch cauliflower and green beans. Drain canned beans. In a mixing bowl, toss together cauliflower, beans, onions, and olives. Chill until just before serving time. In a small bowl, combine oil, vinegar, tarragon, salt, and pepper. Pour over chilled vegetables; toss. Tear lettuce into bite-sized pieces; arrange on a platter. Arrange vegetables over lettuce. Arrange tomato slices and hard-boiled eggs attractively on top.

# Green Salad with Mexican Dressing

Makes 4 servings

- 6 large radishes, sliced
- 1 large tomato, cut in wedges
- 4 to 6 large mushrooms, sliced
- 1 avocado, sliced
- 3 fresh peaches, sliced
- 1/4 head iceberg lettuce, torn into bite-size pieces
- 1/4 head romaine lettuce, torn into bite-size pieces
- Mexican Dressing (below)
- Shredded sharp Cheddar cheese

Arrange vegetables and fruit over lettuce in a large bowl. Add Mexican Dressing; toss and garnish with cheese. Serve immediately.

## Mexican Dressing

Makes 1 1/4 cups

- 1/2 cup mild *or* hot taco sauce
- 1/4 cup red wine vinegar
- 1/4 cup olive oil
- 1 tablespoon minced parsley
- 1 tablespoon diced green chilies
- 1 teaspoon minced cilantro
- 1 teaspoon minced fresh oregano *or* 1/4 teaspoon dried oregano

Combine all ingredients; mix thoroughly. Serve as directed.

# Special Salad

Makes 8 servings

½ cup olive oil
½ cup lemon juice *or* vinegar
¼ teaspoon dry mustard
Salt and pepper to taste
1 romaine lettuce, torn into bite-size pieces
4 tomatoes, cut into wedges
1 green pepper, sliced
1 large red onion, sliced
½ cup chopped fresh parsley
2 hard-boiled eggs, sliced
1 2½-ounce can anchovy fillets
½ cup black olives
¼ pound feta cheese

In a small bowl, combine olive oil, lemon juice, mustard, salt, and pepper; blend well. Place lettuce, tomatoes, green pepper, onion, and parsley in a serving bowl. Add dressing to taste; toss lightly. Add eggs, anchovies, and olives; toss again. Crumble feta cheese over top of salad.

# Spinach Toss

Makes 4 servings

½ cup salad oil
⅓ cup sugar
1 small onion, quartered
3 tablespoons vinegar
2 teaspoons prepared mustard
½ teaspoon celery seed
6 slices bacon, optional
6 cups torn spinach
1 cup sliced fresh mushrooms
2 hard-boiled eggs, chopped

To make dressing, in a blender container, combine oil, sugar, onion, vinegar, mustard, and celery seed. Cover and blend until smooth. Keep covered and chill. If desired, in a skillet fry bacon until crisp; drain and crumble. In a large salad bowl combine spinach, mushrooms, eggs, and bacon, if desired. Pour dressing over salad. Toss lightly.

# Mushroom Salad

Makes 8 servings

1 cup salad oil
4 tablespoons wine vinegar
4 tablespoons fresh lemon juice
Salt and pepper to taste
2 teaspoons basil
1 teaspoon Dijon mustard
¼ teaspoon paprika
2 pounds medium mushrooms
2 cups cherry tomatoes
1 large onion, thinly sliced

In a large glass serving bowl, mix oil, vinegar, lemon juice, salt, and seasonings. Stir in mushrooms, tomatoes, and onion. Chill 8 hours, stirring occasionally.

# Chilled Watercress Soup

Makes 4 servings

- **2 tablespoons butter**
- **1 bunch green onions, chopped**
- **2 tablespoons all-purpose flour**
- **2 tablespoons nonfat dry milk**
- **1 quart half-and-half, at room temperature**
- **2 bunches watercress, roughly chopped (reserve 4 sprigs for garnish)**
- **¼ teaspoon nutmeg**
- **2 teaspoons lemon juice**
- **Salt and pepper to taste**
- **Yogurt**
- **Lemon slices**

Melt butter in saucepan; sauté onion briefly. Stir in flour and dry milk; blend and cook until bubbly. Gradually add half-and-half. Cook, stirring continuously, until soup comes to a boil and thickens. Reduce heat; simmer. Add watercress, nutmeg, and lemon juice. Cover and simmer 3 minutes. Remove soup from heat and whirl in blender until smooth. Season to taste and chill. Garnish each serving with yogurt, a watercress sprig, and lemon slice.

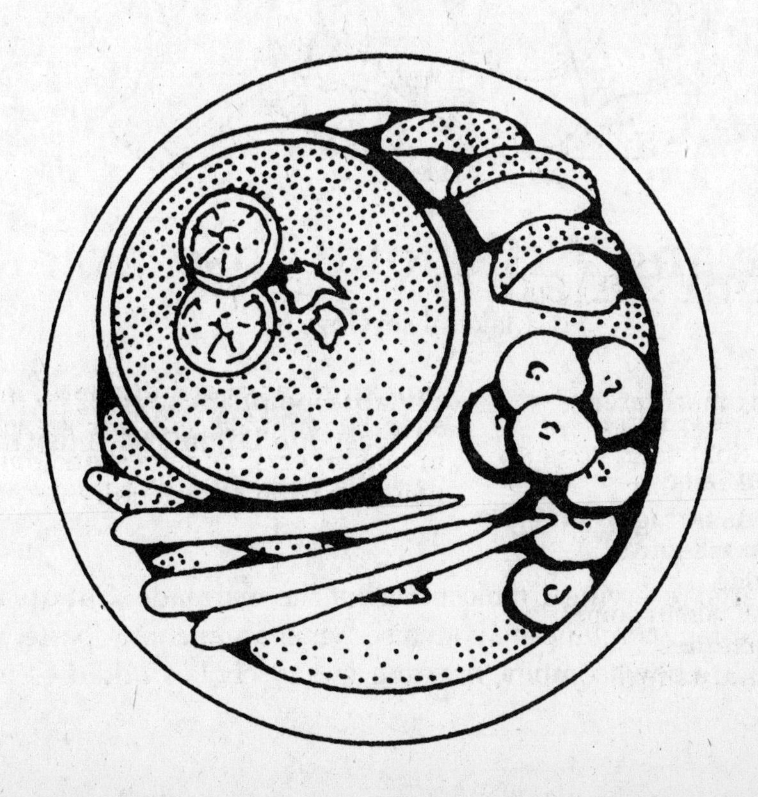

# Tomato-Carrot Salad

Makes 4 servings

- 4 lettuce leaves
- 4 large tomatoes, cut into wedges
- 2 large carrots, grated
- 2/3 cup peanut oil
- Juice and grated rind of one orange
- 1 tablespoon red wine vinegar
- 1 teaspoon Dijon-style mustard
- 1 teaspoon sugar
- Salt and freshly ground black pepper
- Orange wedges

Line 4 bowls with lettuce leaves and top with tomatoes and carrots. Combine remaining ingredients. Pour dressing over each salad just before serving and serve the balance on the side. Garnish with orange wedges.

# Romaine and Artichoke Toss

Makes 4 servings

- 1 6-ounce jar marinated artichoke hearts
- 1/4 cup mayonnaise
- 2 tablespoons tarragon vinegar
- 1 tablespoon anchovy paste
- 1 teaspoon Dijon-style mustard
- 3 cups torn romaine

Drain artichoke hearts, reserving 2 tablespoons of the marinade. Cut up artichokes; set aside. To make dressing, combine mayonnaise, vinegar, anchovy paste, mustard, and reserved marinade. In a bowl combine romaine and artichokes; add dressing and toss.

# Vegetables

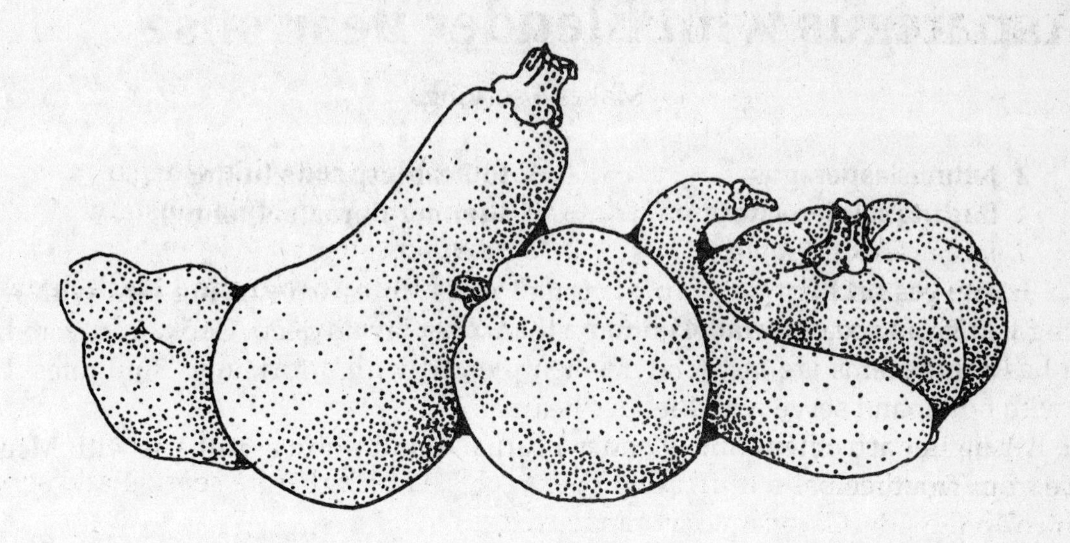

## Herbed Squash and Mushrooms

Makes 4 servings

- 1 pound (4 small) crookneck *or* zucchini squash, quartered
- 1/2 pound mushrooms, halved
- 1/4 cup chicken broth
- 1/2 teaspoon dried basil or tarragon
- Salt and pepper to taste

Place all ingredients in a skillet; cover and simmer until tender-crisp, 6 to 8 minutes.

## Sliced Beefsteak Tomatoes

Makes 4 servings

- 3 large beefsteak tomatoes
- 1/3 cup olive oil
- 1/4 cup lemon juice
- 1 tablespoon chopped fresh basil *or* 1/2 teaspoon dried basil
- 1 tablespoon freshly chopped rosemary *or* 1/2 teaspoon dried rosemary

Slice tomatoes. Whisk together remaining ingredients; pour over tomatoes. Let stand at room temperature until serving.

# Asparagus with Blender Bearnaise

Makes 4 servings

**2 pounds asparagus**
**Boiling salted water**
**1 to 2 tablespoons butter**
**Blender Bernaise(below)**

Wash asparagus and cut or snap off tough ends. In a wide frying pan with a little boiling water, lay spears parallel no more than three layers deep. Cook, uncovered, over high heat until stems are just tender when pierced with a fork, 6 to 8 minutes. Drain. Top with butter and serve with Blender Bearnaise.
*Note:* For lighter appetites, omit Blender Bearnaise and serve asparagus with Meuniere Sauce from Trout recipe.

## Blender Bearnaise

Makes 1 cup

**1/4 cup wine vinegar**
**1/4 cup vermouth *or* white wine**
**1 shallot *or* green onion, minced**
**1 teaspoon dried tarragon leaves**
**1 bay leaf**
**6 black peppercorns**
**6 parsley sprigs**
**1 cup butter**
**3 egg yolks**

In a small saucepan bring first 7 ingredients to a boil; reduce to 3 tablespoons. Melt butter in a separate saucepan. In blender whirl yolks until just blended. Add reduced wine mixture and blend briefly. Add melted butter, a droplet at a time, blending continuously on high speed. As mixture thickens, increase butter to a thin stream. Keep sauce warm by placing blender container in a pan of lukewarm water, if desired.
*Note:* For a faster Hollandaise version, simply omit first 7 ingredients and the first step. Proceed as directed. Makes 1/2 cup.

## Curry Bearnaise Variation

Makes 1 cup

**1 tablespoon vegetable oil**
**1/2 small onion, chopped**
**1 tablespoon curry powder**
**3/4 cup plain yogurt**

Heat oil in skillet; sauté onion until tender. Stir in curry; cook 3 to 4 minutes, stirring constantly. Transfer to a blender or food processor. Add yogurt; blend until smooth.

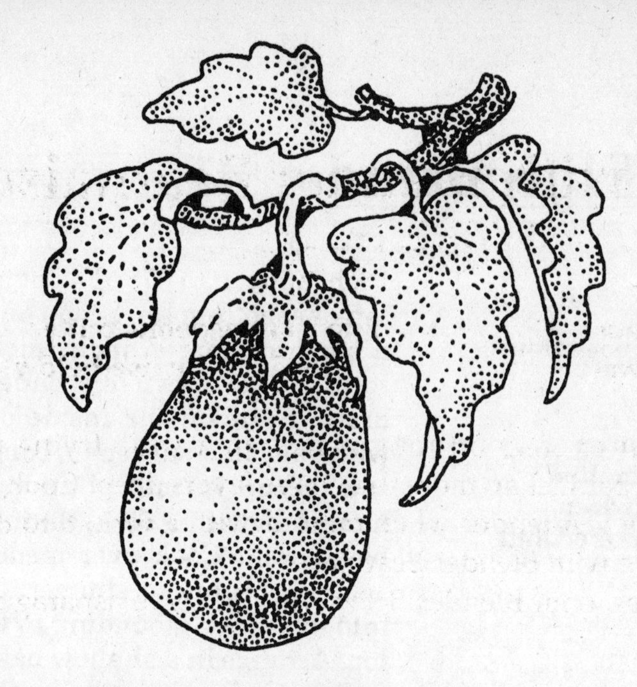

# Eggplant Parmigiana

Makes 6 servings

**1 cup olive oil**
**1 large eggplant *or* two small eggplants, peeled and cut into ½-inch slices**
**1¼ cups Tomato Sauce**
**6 tablespoons grated Parmesan cheese**
**½ pound mozzarella cheese, thinly sliced**

Preheat oven to 400° F. In a large, heavy skillet, heat oil. Fry eggplant in hot oil until lightly browned; drain. In a flat casserole, arrange 1 layer of the fried eggplant. Cover with Tomato Sauce. Sprinkle with Parmesan cheese; top with a layer of mozzarella. Repeat procedure until all the eggplant is used, ending with a layer of mozzarella. Bake for 15 minutes. Serve hot.

# Tomato Sauce

Makes 2½ quarts

**3 tablespoons olive oil**
**½ stalk celery, finely chopped**
**1 onion, chopped**
**1 teaspoon minced fresh parsley**
**1 clove garlic, minced**
**1 28-ounce can Italian tomatoes**
**1 6-ounce can tomato puree**
**2 bay leaves**
**½ teaspoon salt**
**½ teaspoon basil**
**½ teaspoon pepper**
**½ teaspoon oregano**

In a medium saucepan over medium heat, heat oil. Add celery, onion, parsley, and garlic; sauté until vegetables are tender, stirring often. Add tomatoes and tomato puree. Stir in seasonings. Simmer gently, uncovered, for 40 minutes, stirring occasionally. Remove bay leaves before serving.

# Tomatoes Florentine

Makes 8 servings

- 8 medium tomatoes
- Salt
- 2 tablespoons all-purpose flour
- ½ teaspoon salt
- ¼ cup milk
- 1 egg yolk, lightly beaten
- 1 tablespoon butter, melted
- 1 10-ounce package frozen chopped spinach, cooked and drained

Preheat oven to 375° F. Cut a slice from the top of each tomato. Scoop out pulp, leaving a shell at least ¼ inch thick. Place tomatoes upside down on paper toweling to drain. Sprinkle the inside of each tomato with salt. In a saucepan, combine flour and salt. Blend in milk. Stir in egg yolk and melted butter. Add well-drained spinach; blend well. Cook over medium heat until spinach begins to simmer. Spoon mixture into tomatoes, mounding to form a rounded top. Arrange in a shallow baking dish. Bake for 10-15 minutes until tomatoes are cooked but not mushy. Serve hot.

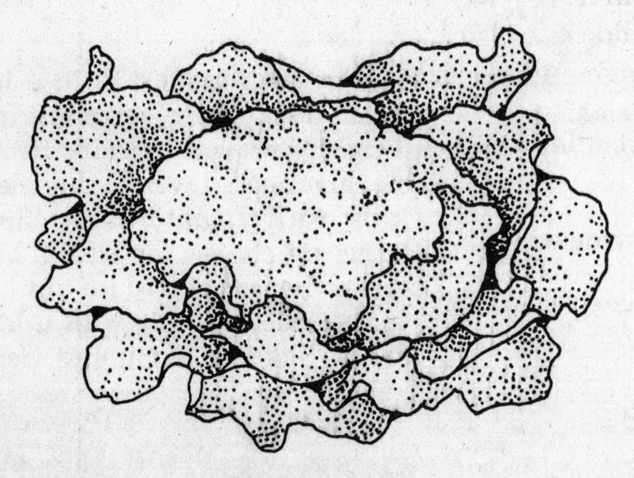

# Golden Cauliflower

Makes 4 servings

- 2 tablespoons butter *or* margarine
- 4 cups thinly sliced cauliflower
- ⅓ cup water
- 1 cup shredded Cheddar cheese
- 1 teaspoon paprika

Melt butter *or* margarine in large skillet; add cauliflower and water. Cover and steam over high heat for 3 minutes. Sprinkle with cheese and paprika; cover and continue steaming until cheese melts and cauliflower is tender, about 2 minutes.